The Supporters' Guide to Irish Football 1997

EDITOR
John Robinson

First Edition

CONTENTS

Foreword 3
Irish F.A. Information 4
Smirnoff Premier & 1st Division Clubs 5-20
Wilkinson Sword 'B' Division Section 1 Clubs 21-36
Northern Ireland Statistics 1995-96 37-42
League of Ireland Information 43
Harp Lager National League Premier Clubs 44-55
Harp Lager National League 1st Division Clubs 56-65
Republic of Ireland Statistics 1995-96 66-70
Previous Supporters' Guides 71
The 25 Year Records 72

British Library Cataloguing in Publication Data
A catalogue record for this book is available from the British Library
ISBN 0-947808-87-6

Copyright © 1996; SOCCER BOOK PUBLISHING LTD. (01472-696226)
72, St. Peters' Avenue, Cleethorpes, N.E. Lincolnshire, DN35 8HU, England

All rights are reserved. No part of this publication may be reproduced, stored into a retrieval system or transmitted, in any form or by any means, electronic, mechanical, photocopying, recording, or otherwise, without the prior written permission of Soccer Book Publishing Ltd.

The Publishers, and the Football Clubs itemised are unable to accept liability for any loss, damage or injury caused by error or inaccuracy in the information published in this guide.

Printed by Adlard Print & Typesetting Services, The Old School, The Green, Ruddington, Notts. NG11 6HH

FOREWORD

It has taken over three years to gather together the information to enable us to publish this guide and we are indebted to the following people for their invaluable assistance: – Kevin Norminton (photos), Gerry Desmond (Republic Stats. and information), Marshall Gillespie (Northern Ireland Stats. and information), John Quinn (Irish F.A.), Tony Butler (F.A. of Ireland), Ceri Sampson (cover design), Michael Robinson and Paul Bruce (page layouts) and the many club officials who have taken so much trouble to provide information.

We make no political statement in combining clubs from Northern Ireland and the Republic of Ireland into a single guide – in view of the relatively small number of clubs involved – this is the only way that we can produce a value-for-money publication!

Finally, we would like to wish our readers a happy and safe spectating season.

John Robinson

EDITOR

IRISH FOOTBALL ASSOCIATION

Founded
1880

Address
20 Windsor Avenue,
Belfast, BT9 6EG

Phone (01232) 669458
Fax (01232) 667620

Contents
Smirnoff Premier & 1st Division Clubs
Wilkinson Sword 'B' Division Section '1' Clubs

ARDS FC

Founded: 1902
Former Name(s): Ards United
Nickname: The Red & Blues
Ground: Castlereagh Park, Newtownards, Co. Down.
Record Attendance: 11,500
Colours: Shirts - Red & Blue Stripes
    Shorts - Red & Blue
Contact No.: (01247) 813370

Pitch Size: 111 x 66 yds
Ground Capacity: 10,000
Seating Capacity: 550
Correspondence Address:
Secretary: K. Lowry, 20 East Mount, Newtownards, Co. Down, BT23 5SE
Contact No.: (01247) 817562 (Home), (01247) 812113 (Business)

GENERAL INFORMATION
Supporters Club Administrator: None
Address:
Telephone Number:
Car Parking: At Ground
Coach Parking: At Ground
Nearest Railway Station: Bangor (8 mls)
Nearest Bus Station: Newtownards
Club Shop: Yes
Opening Times: Match Days Only
Telephone No.: (01247) 813370
Postal Sales: Yes
Nearest Police Station: Newtownards
Police Force: RUC
Police Telephone No.: (01247) 818080

DISABLED SUPPORTERS INFORMATION
Wheelchairs: Accommodated
Disabled Toilets: None
The Blind: No special facilities

ADMISSION INFO (1996/97 PRICES)
Adult Standing: £5.00
Adult Seating: £6.50
Child Standing: £3.00
Child Seating: £4.00
Concessionary Standing: £3.00
Concessionary Seating: £4.00
Programme Price: £1.00
FAX Number: (01247) 819549 or (01247) 826004

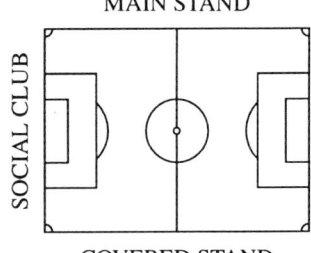

Travelling Supporters Information:
Routes: Take the A20 from Belfast or the A21 from Bangor into town centre then take the Portaferry Road for the ground

BALLYCLARE COMRADES FC

Founded: 1919
Former Name(s) : None
Nickname: The Comrades
Ground: Dixon Park, Ballyclare, Co.Antrim.
Record Attendance: Not known
Colours: Shirts - Red & White
  Shorts - Red & Black
Contact No.: (019603) 52319
Pitch Size: 110 x 72 yds

Ground Capacity: 4,500
Seating Capacity: 200
Correspondence Address: D. A. Horner, 20 Heather Park, Ballyclare, Co. Antrim
Contact No.: (019603) 23480
Social Club Phone: (019603) 22945

GENERAL INFORMATION
Supporters Club Administrator: None
Address: –
Telephone Number: –
Car Parking: Street parking only
Coach Parking: By Police Direction
Nearest Railway Station: Carrickfergus (8 miles)
Nearest Bus Station: Ballyclare
Club Shop: None
Opening Times: None
Telephone No.: –
Postal Sales: –
Nearest Police Station: Ballyclare
Police Force: RUC
Police Telephone No.: (01232) 650222

DISABLED SUPPORTERS INFORMATION
Wheelchairs: Acommodated
Disabled Toilets: None
The Blind: No Special Facilities

ADMISSION INFO (1996/97 PRICES)
Adult Standing: £4.00
Adult Seating: £5.00
Child Standing: £3.00
Child Seating: £3.00
Concessionary Standing: £3.00
Concessionary Seating: £3.00
Programme Price: None
FAX Number: None

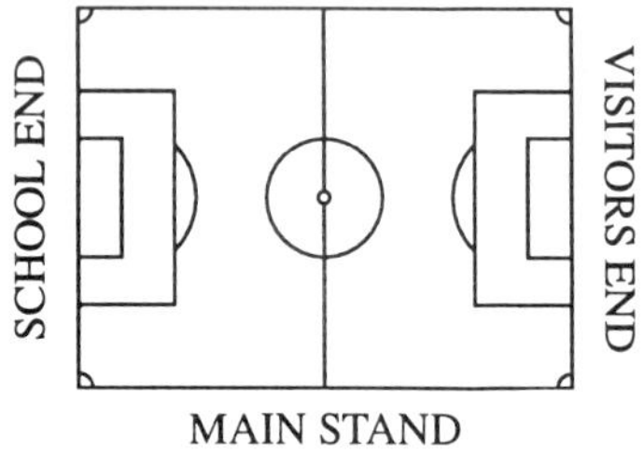

SCHOOL END / VISITORS END / MAIN STAND

Travelling Supporters Information:
Routes: Exit M2 at junction 5 and take the A57 to Ballyclare. Ground is easily found in town centre adjacent to the supermarket but parking nearby may be a problem.

BALLYMENA UNITED FC

Founded: 1928
Former Name(s): None
Nickname: United
Ground: The Showgrounds, Warden Street, Ballymena, Co. Antrim.
Record Attendance: Not known
Colours: Shirts - Sky Blue & White
Shorts - White
Phone No.: (01266) 652049

Pitch Size: 109 x 70 yds
Ground Capacity: 8,000
Seating Capacity: 2,000
Correspondence Address: D. Stirling, 37 Queen St, Ballymena, Co. Antrim, BT42 1BD
Contact No.: (01266) 659490 (Business)
Social Club Phone: (01266) 656219

GENERAL INFORMATION
Supporters Club Administrator: None
Address:
Telephone Number:
Car Parking: At Ground
Coach Parking: At Ground
Nearest Railway Station: Ballymena (1 ml)
Nearest Bus Station: Ballymena
Club Shop: Yes
Opening Times: Matchdays
Telephone No.:
Postal Sales:
Nearest Police Station: Ballymena
Police Force: RUC
Police Telephone No.: (01266) 653355

DISABLED SUPPORTERS INFORMATION
Wheelchairs: Accommodated
Disabled Toilets: Yes
The Blind: No Special Facilities

ADMISSION INFO (1996/97 PRICES)
Adult Standing: £4.00
Adult Seating: £5.00
Child Standing: £2.00
Child Seating: £3.00
Programme Price: None
FAX Number: None

MAIN STAND

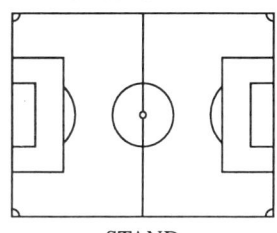

STAND

Travelling Supporters Information:
Routes: Take the A26 into Ballymena. In Town centre at junction of A43 & A42 turn off at roundabout into Warden Street. Ground about 0.25 ml at end of Road.

BANGOR FC

Founded: 1918
Former Name(s): None
Nickname: The Seasiders
Ground: Clandeboye Park, Clandeboye Road, Bangor, Co. Down.
Record Attendance: Not known
Colours: Shirts - Gold
         Shorts - Royal Blue
Phone No.: (01247) 457712

Pitch Size: 105 x 60 yds
Ground Capacity: 5,000
Seating Capacity: 1,000
Correspondence Address: F. Anderson, 2 Belmont Drive, Bangor, Co. Down, BT19 1NH
Contact No.: (01247) 469826 (Home)
(01232) 321212 (Business)
Social Club Phone: (01247) 462802

GENERAL INFORMATION
Supporters Club Administrator: None
Address: -
Telephone Number: -
Car Parking: At Ground
Coach Parking: At Ground
Nearest Railway Station: Bangor (1 ml)
Nearest Bus Station: Bangor
Club Shop: In Social Club
Opening Times: Club Hours /Matchdays
Telephone No.: -
Postal Sales: -
Nearest Police Station: Bangor
Police Force: RUC
Police Telephone No.: (01247) 454444

DISABLED SUPPORTERS INFORMATION
Wheelchairs: Accommodated
Disabled Toilets: Yes
The Blind: No Special Facilities

ADMISSION INFO (1996/97 PRICES)
Adult Standing: £4.00
Adult Seating: £5.00
Child Standing: £2.00
Child Seating: £3.00
Programme Price: £1.00
FAX Number: (01247) 457712

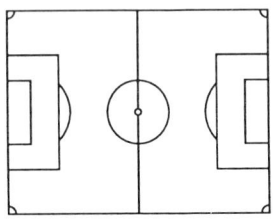

MAIN STAND

COVERED TERRACING

Travelling Supporters Information:
Routes: Take the A2 to Bangor and just before Town Centre take right at traffic lights directly after Railway Bridge. Drive past Church then turn right into Clandeboye Road and ground is 0.25 mile on right.

CARRICK RANGERS FC

Founded: 1939
Former Name(s): None
Nickname: Rangers
Ground: Taylors Avenue, Carrickfergus, Co. Antrim.
Record Attendance: Not Known
Colours: Shirts - Amber & Black
Shorts - Black
Phone No.: (019603) 51009

Pitch Size: 105 x 68 yds
Ground Capacity: 5,000
Seating Capacity: 750
Correspondence Address: G. Wright, 85 B Salia Avenue, Carrickfergus BT38 8NE
Contact No.: (019603) 849140 (Business)
(019603) 69059 (Home)
Social Club No.: (019603) 63946

GENERAL INFORMATION
Supporters Club Administrator: Andrew McKeever
Address: c/o Club
Telephone Number: (019603) 51009
Car Parking: At Ground
Coach Parking: At Ground
Nearest Railway Station: Carrickfergus
Nearest Bus Station: Carrickfergus
Club Shop: Yes
Opening Times: Matchdays only
Telephone No.: (019603) 51009
Postal Sales: Yes
Nearest Police Station: Carrickfergus
Police Force: RUC
Police Telephone No.: (01232) 650222

DISABLED SUPPORTERS INFORMATION
Wheelchairs: Accommodated
Disabled Toilets: Yes
The Blind: None

ADMISSION INFO (1996/97 PRICES)
Adult Standing: £4.00
Adult Seating: £5.00
Child Standing: £3.00
Child Seating: £3.00
Concessionary Standing: £3.00
Concessionary Seating: £3.00
Programme Price: 60p
FAX Number: None

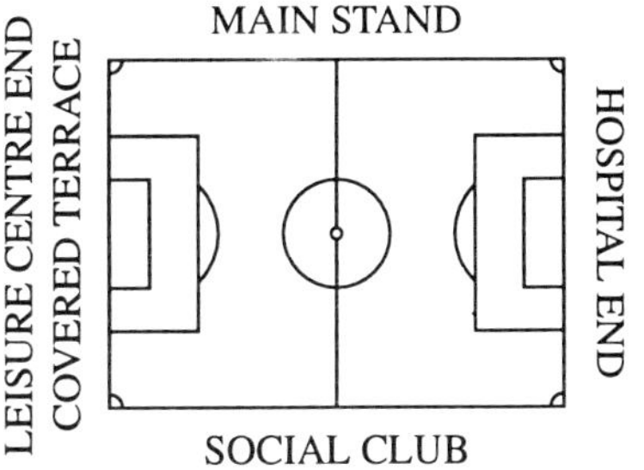

Travelling Supporters Information:
Routes: Take the A2 to Carrickfergus. Ground is just off Sea Front adjacent to Health Centre.

CLIFTONVILLE FC

Founded: 1879
Former Name(s): None
Nickname: The Reds
Ground: Solitude, Cliftonville Street, Belfast, BT14.
Record Attendance: 28,600
Colours: Shirts - Red
  Shorts - White

Phone No.: (01232) 754628
Pitch Size: 135 x 72 yds
Ground Capacity: 8,000
Seating Capacity: 1,100
Correspondence Address:
John Duffy, c/o club
Contact No.: (01232) 717777

GENERAL INFORMATION
Supporters Club Administrator: Murray
Address: c/o Club
Telephone Number: (01232) 754628
Car Parking: Street parking only
Coach Parking: By Police Direction
Nearest Railway Station: Belfast
Nearest Bus Station: Belfast
Club Shop: Yes
Opening Times: Matchdays only
Telephone No.: (01232) 754628
Postal Sales: Yes
Nearest Police Station: Old Park, Belfast
Police Force: RUC
Police Telephone No.: (01232) 650222

DISABLED SUPPORTERS INFORMATION
Wheelchairs: Accommodated
Disabled Toilets: None
The Blind: No Special Facilities

ADMISSION INFO (1996/97 PRICES)
Adult Standing: £5.00
Adult Seating: £6.00
Child Standing: £3.00
Child Seating: £3.00
Concessionary Standing: £3.00
Concessionary Seating: £3.00
Programme Price: £1.00
FAX Number: None

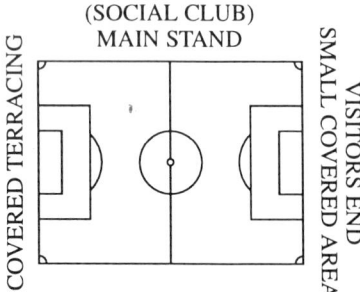

Travelling Supporters Information:
Routes: The ground is situated in the North of Belfast in Cliftonville Street. Exit M2 onto A12 Ring Road and turn right into Clifton Street. Continue into Antrim Road at Carlisle Circus. Turn left at College into Cliftonville Road and ground is on right after Primary School.

COLERAINE FC

Founded: 1927
Former Name(s): Coleraine Alexandra & Coleraine Olympic amalgamated in 1927
Nickname: Bannsiders
Ground: The Showgrounds, Coleraine, Co. Londonderry.
Record Attendance: 12,500
Colours: Shirts - Blue & White Stripes
Shorts - White
Phone No.: (01265) 53655

Pitch Size: 120 x 80 yds
Ground Capacity: 12,500
Seating Capacity: 2,000
Correspondence Address: F. Monahan, 10 Waterford Drive, Coleraine, Co. Londonderry, BT52 1NQ
Contact No.: (01265) 43685 (Home) (01265) 53303 (Business)
Social Club No.: (01265) 42571

GENERAL INFORMATION
Supporters Club Administrator: None
Address: –
Telephone Number: –
Car Parking: At Ground
Coach Parking: Adjacent
Nearest Railway Station: Coleraine (0.25 mile)
Nearest Bus Station: Coleraine (0.25 mile)
Club Shop: Yes
Opening Times: Matchdays only
Telephone No.: None
Postal Sales: Yes
Nearest Police Station: Lodge Rd. Coleraine
Police Force: RUC
Police Telephone No.: (01265) 44122

DISABLED SUPPORTERS INFORMATION
Wheelchairs: Accommodated
Disabled Toilets: Yes
The Blind: No Special Facilities

ADMISSION INFO (1996/97 PRICES)
Adult Standing: £4.00
Adult Seating: £6.00
Child Standing: £2.00
Child Seating: £3.00
Concessionary Standing: £2.00
Concessionary Seating: £3.00
Programme Price: £1.00
FAX Number: (01265) 329188

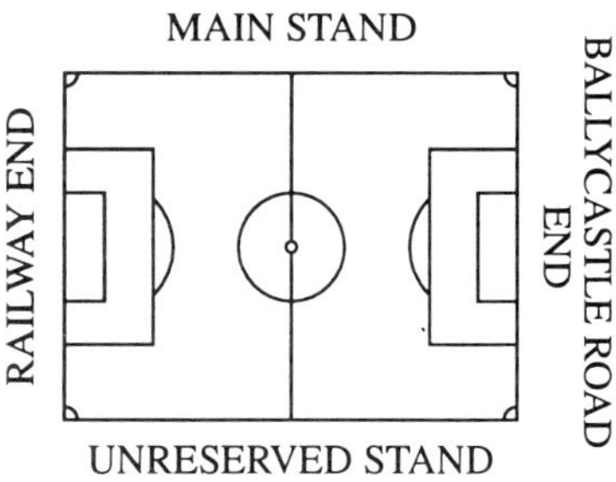

```
              MAIN STAND
         ┌─────────────────┐
    R    │                 │   B
    A    │                 │   A
    I    │                 │   L
    L    │                 │   L
    W    │       ◯         │   Y
    A    │                 │   C
    Y    │                 │   A
         │                 │   S
    E    │                 │   T
    N    │                 │   L
    D    │                 │   E
         │                 │
         │                 │   R
         │                 │   O
         │                 │   A
         │                 │   D
         └─────────────────┘
                             E
                             N
                             D
          UNRESERVED STAND
```

Travelling Supporters Information:
Routes: Take the A26 to Coleraine and join Ring Road heading towards Portrush. At "Ballycastle Road Roundabout" signposts leave Ring Road and follow Town Centre signs. Ground is approximately 0.6 mile on left.

CRUSADERS FC

Founded: 1898
Former Name(s): None
Nickname: Hatchet Men
Ground: Seaview, Shore Road, Belfast, BT15 3PL
Record Attendance: 11,000
Colours: Shirts - Red & Black Stripes
Shorts - White
Phone No.: (01232) 370777

Pitch Size: 108 x 72 yds
Ground Capacity: 9,000
Seating Capacity: 1,000
Correspondence Address: H. Davison, 23 Oakmount Drive, Belfast, BT15 3RE
Contact No.: (01232) 775831 (Home)

GENERAL INFORMATION
Supporters Club Administrator: None
Address: –
Telephone Number: –
Car Parking: Street Parking
Coach Parking: At Ground
Nearest Railway Station: Belfast
Nearest Bus Station: Belfast
Club Shop: Yes
Opening Times: Matchdays only
Telephone No.: (01232) 370777
Postal Sales: Yes
Nearest Police Station: York Road, Belfast
Police Force: RUC
Police Telephone No.: (01232) 650222

DISABLED SUPPORTERS INFORMATION
Wheelchairs: Accommodated
Disabled Toilets: None
The Blind: No Special Facilities

ADMISSION INFO (1996/97 PRICES)
Adult Standing: £5.00
Adult Seating: £6.00
Child Standing: £3.00
Child Seating: £4.00
Concessionary Standing: £3.00
Concessionary Seating: £4.00
Programme Price: £1.00
FAX Number: (01232) 771049

MAIN STAND

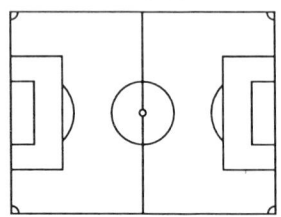

COVERED TERRACING

Travelling Supporters Information:
Routes: Exit M2 at junction 1 and take the Shore Road Southwards. Ground is 0.25 mile on left.

DISTILLERY FC

Founded: 1879
Former Name(s): None
Nickname: Whites
Ground: New Grosvenor Stadium, Ballyskeagh, Lambeg, Lisburn, Co. Antrim.
Record Attendance: Not known
Colours: Shirts - White & Dark Blue
Shorts - White

Phone No.: (01232) 301148
Pitch Size: 110 x 72 yds
Ground Capacity: 7,000
Seating Capacity: 5,000
Correspondence Address:
Mr. C. Oakes, c/o Club
Social Club No.: (01232) 620178

GENERAL INFORMATION
Supporters Club Administrator: None
Address: –
Telephone Number: –
Car Parking: At Ground
Coach Parking: At Ground
Nearest Railway Station: Lambeg (1 mile)
Nearest Bus Station: Lisburn
Club Shop: Yes at Social Club
Opening Times: Match days only
Telephone No.: (01232) 620178
Postal Sales: Yes
Nearest Police Station: Lisburn
Police Force: RUC
Police Telephone No.: (01232) 650222

DISABLED SUPPORTERS INFORMATION
Wheelchairs: Accommodation
Disabled Toilets: None
The Blind: No Special Facilities

ADMISSION INFO (1996/97 PRICES)
Adult Standing: £4.00
Adult Seating: £5.00
Child Standing: £3.00
Child Seating: £3.00
Concessionary Standing: £3.00
Concessionary Seating: £3.00
Programme Price: £1.00
FAX Number: None

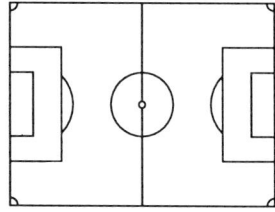

MAIN STAND

COVERED SIDE
(SOCIAL CLUB)

Travelling Supporters Information:
Routes: Exit M1 at Junction 6 and take the A49 to Lisburn. Then take the A1 Belfast Road to Lambeg Railway Station and turn off by the station. Continue along past the Golf club and ground is on right (about 1 mile from railway station)

GLENAVON FC

Founded: 1889
Former Name(s): Lurgan Glenavon F.C.
Nickname: Lurgan Blues
Ground: Mourneview Park, Mourneview Ave.
Lurgan, Co. Antrim, BT66 8EW
Record Attendance: Not known
Colours: Shirts - Royal Blue
        Shorts - White

Phone No.: (01762) 322472
Pitch Size: 109 x 76yds
Ground Capacity: 10,971
Seating Capacity: 1,247
Correspondence Address: c/o Club
Social Club No.: (01762) 323307

GENERAL INFORMATION
Supporters Club Administrator: None
Address: –
Telephone Number: –
Car Parking: At Ground & Street Parking
Coach Parking: At Ground
Nearest Railway Station: Lurgan
Nearest Bus Station: Lurgan
Club Shop: Yes
Opening Times: Matchdays
Telephone No.: (01762) 330406
Postal Sales: Yes
Nearest Police Station: Lurgan
Police Force: RUC
Police Telephone No.: (01762) 325144

DISABLED SUPPORTERS INFORMATION
Wheelchairs: Accommodated in disabled section
Disabled Toilets: Yes
The Blind: No Special Facilities

ADMISSION INFO (1996/97 PRICES)
Adult Standing: £5.00
Adult Seating: £7.00
Child Standing: £3.50
Child Seating: £4.50
Concessionary Standing: £3.50
Concessionary Seating: £4.50
Programme Price: £1.00
FAX Number: (01762) 327694

MAIN STAND

COVERED END

COVERED TERRACE

Travelling Supporters Information:
Routes: Exit M1 at junction 10 and take the A26 to Lurgan. Travel to Queen Street Junction and turn left into Malcolm Road. Join Russell Drive, then turn left at Lurgan Hospital into Tandragee Road. Turn left at Mourneview Avenue junction and Ground is on left.

GLENTORAN FC

Founded: 1882
Former Name(s): None
Nickname: The Glens
Ground: The Oval, Mersey Street, Belfast, BT4 1FG.
Record Attendance: 40,000
Colours: Shirts - Green, Black & Red
Shorts - Black

Phone No.: (01232) 456137
Pitch Size: 112 x 72 yds
Ground Capacity: 30,000
Seating Capacity: 3,000
Correspondence Address:
J. Warren c/o Club
Social Club No.: (01232) 457670

GENERAL INFORMATION
Supporters Club Administrator: P. Millar
Address: c/o club
Telephone Number: (01232) 456137
Car Parking: Street Parking
Coach Parking: At Ground
Nearest Railway Station: Belfast
Nearest Bus Station: Belfast
Club Shop: Yes
Opening Times: Weekdays & Matchdays
Telephone No.: (01232) 456137
Postal Sales: Yes
Nearest Police Station: Mountpottinger
Police Force: RUC
Police Telephone No.: (01232) 650222

DISABLED SUPPORTERS INFORMATION
Wheelchairs: Accommodated In Disabled Section
Disabled Toilets: Yes
The Blind: No Special Facilities

ADMISSION INFO (1996/97 PRICES)
Adult Standing: £5.00
Adult Seating: £6.00
Child Standing: £3.00
Child Seating: £4.00
Concessionary Standing: £3.00
Concessionary Seating: £4.00
Programme Price: £1.00
FAX Number: (01232) 732956

```
             MAIN STAND
      ┌─────────────────────┐
  O   │                     │   O
  P   │   ┌─┐         ┌─┐   │   P
  E   │   │ │    ○    │ │   │   E
  N   │   └─┘         └─┘   │   N
      │                     │
  T   │                     │   T
  E   │                     │   E
  R   │                     │   R
  R   │                     │   R
  A   │                     │   A
  C   │                     │   C
  E   │                     │   E
      └─────────────────────┘
           COVERED TERRACE
```

Travelling Supporters Information:
Routes: Exit M3 at junction with A2 and follow signs for A20 (Newtownards Road). After junction with Bridge Road, turn left into Coniswater Street and continue into Severn Street. Take any right turn for Ground.

LARNE FC

Founded: 1900
Former Name(s): Larne Olympic FC
Nickname: None
Ground: Inver Park, Larne, Co. Antrim
Record Attendance: Not known
Colours: Shirts - Red with White facings
Shorts - White
Phone No.: (01574) 74292

Pitch Size: 110 x 66 yds
Ground Capacity: 12,000
Seating Capacity: 600
Correspondence Address: R.F. Orr,
18 Mountcoole Gardens, Belfast, BT14 8JB
Contact No.: (01232) 715558

GENERAL INFORMATION
Supporters Club Administrator: None
Address: –
Telephone Number: –
Car Parking: Street Parking
Coach Parking: At Ground
Nearest Railway Station: Larne
Nearest Bus Station: Larne
Club Shop: Yes
Opening Times: Matchdays only
Telephone No.: –
Postal Sales: –
Nearest Police Station: Larne
Police Force: RUC
Police Telephone No.: (01232) 650222

DISABLED SUPPORTERS INFORMATION
Wheelchairs: Accommodated
Disabled Toilets: None
The Blind: No Special Facilities

ADMISSION INFO (1996/97 PRICES)
Adult Standing: £4.00
Adult Seating: £5.00
Child Standing: £2.00
Child Seating: £2.00
Concessionary Standing: £2.00
Concessionary Seating: £3.00
Programme Price: £1.00
FAX Number: None

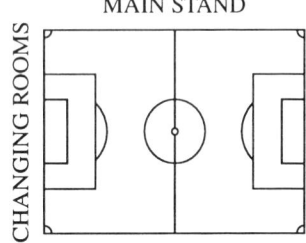

Travelling Supporters Information:
Routes: Take the A2 or the A8 to Larne, then at large roundabout in Town Centre, take the Carrickfergus Road and follow signs for 'Inver' for Ground.

LINFIELD FC

Founded: 1886
Former Name(s): None
Nickname: The Blues
Ground: Windsor Park, Donegall Ave, Belfast, BT12 6LW
Record Attendance: 58,000
Colours: Shirts - Royal Blue
    Shorts - White

Phone No.: (01232) 244198
Pitch Size: 110 x 75 yds
Ground Capacity: 28,500
Seating Capacity: 10,500
Correspondence Address: c/o Club

GENERAL INFORMATION
Supporters Club Administrator: None
Address: c/o Club
Telephone Number: (01232) 244198
Car Parking: At Ground & Street Parking
Coach Parking: At Ground
Nearest Railway Station: Belfast
Nearest Bus Station: Belfast
Club Shop: Yes – behind South Stand & Sports shop in Donegall Ave
Opening Times: Matchdays & Shop Hours
Telephone No.: (01232) 244198
Postal Sales: Yes
Nearest Police Station: Lisburn Road
Police Force: RUC
Police Telephone No. (01232) 650222

DISABLED SUPPORTERS INFORMATION
Wheelchairs: Accommodated
Disabled Toilets: Yes
The Blind: No Special Facilities

ADMISSION INFO (1996/97 PRICES)
Adult Seating: £6.00
Child Seating: £3.00
Concessionary Seating: £3.00 or £4.00
Programme Price: £1.00
FAX Number: (01232) 744691
Note: Only seating sections are used for most games

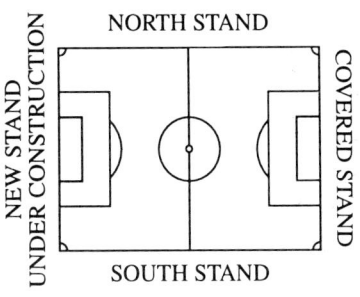

Travelling Supporters Information:
Routes: Exit M1 Junction 1 and follow signs into Donegall Road. Just before railway bridge turn right into Donegall Avenue and ground is 0.25 mile on right.

NEWRY TOWN FC

Founded: 1923
Former Name(s):
Nickname: The Town
Ground: The Showgrounds, Newry, Co. Down.
Record Attendance: Not known
Colours: Shirts - Blue & White Stripes
Shorts - White
Phone No.: (01693) 64551

Pitch Size: 110 x 75yds
Ground Capacity: 5,000
Seating Capacity: 100
Correspondence Address:
Mr. McVicar, c/o Club

GENERAL INFORMATION
Supporters Club Administrator: None
Address: c/o Club
Telephone Number: (01693) 64551
Car Parking: At Ground
Coach Parking: At Ground
Nearest Railway Station: Newry
Nearest Bus Station: Newry
Club Shop: Yes
Opening Times: Match Days Only
Telephone No.: None
Postal Sales: None
Nearest Police Station: Newry
Police Force: RUC
Police Telephone No.: (01693) 65500

DISABLED SUPPORTERS INFORMATION
Wheelchairs: Accommodated
Disabled Toilets: None
The Blind: No Special Facilities

ADMISSION INFO (1996/97 PRICES)
Adult Standing: £4.00
Adult Seating: £5.00
Child Standing: £3.00
Child Seating: £4.00
Concessionary Standing: £3.00
Concessionary Seating: £4.00
Programme Price: £1.00
FAX Number: None

COVERED TERRACE

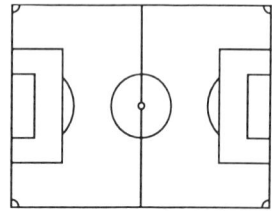

OPEN TERRACE

Travelling Supporters Information:
Routes: The ground is situated to the South of Newry just off the A2 bypass. Travelling from Newry, turn right at large roundabout signposted Green Bank Industrial Estate and ground is adjacent to Gaelic Football ground on right.

OMAGH TOWN FC

Founded: 1962
Former Name(s): Omagh Celtic FC (1962-69)
Nickname: The Town
Ground: St. Julians Road, Mullaghmore, Omagh, Co. Tyrone.
Record Attendance: 3,020 (1993)
Colours: Shirts - White
Shorts - Black
Phone No.: (01662) 242223 (Club Office)

Pitch Size: 112 x 72yds
Ground Capacity: 8,000
Seating Capacity: 400
Correspondence Address: P. McGlinchey, 16 D Sedan Avenue, Omagh, Co. Tyrone, BT79 7AQ
Contact No.: (01662) 242927 (Ground)
(01662) 243228 (Press)

GENERAL INFORMATION
Supporters Club Administrator: N. Boyle
Address: 16D Sedan Ave, Omagh, Co. Tyrone
Telephone Number: (01662) 242233
Car Parking: At Ground
Coach Parking: At Ground
Nearest Railway Station: Derry 34 miles – North; Portatown 40 miles – South
Nearest Bus Station: Omagh (1 mile)
Club Shop: Yes-In Social Club and at ground
Opening Times: Club Hours 11.30-11.30pm
Telephone No.: (01662) 242223
Postal Sales: Yes
Nearest Police Station: Omagh (0.5 miles)
Police Force: RUC
Police Telephone No.: (01662) 246177

DISABLED SUPPORTERS INFORMATION
Wheelchairs: Accommodated
Disabled Toilets: None
The Blind: No Special Facilities

ADMISSION INFO (1996/97 PRICES)
Adult Standing: £4.45
Adult Seating: £5.00
Child Standing: Free
Child Seating: Free
Concessionary Standing: £2.00
Concessionary Seating: £2.50
Programme Price: £1.00
FAX Number: (01662) 242927

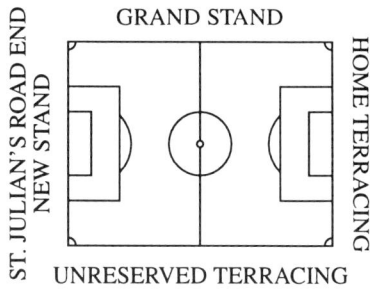

Travelling Supporters Information:
Routes: From Belfast take M1 to end then take A4 to Ballygawley to A5. Take A5 to Omagh town centre then follow Gortin Road to Killybrack Road and follow this into St. Julian's Road for ground; From Londonderry Take A5 to town centre then as above.

PORTADOWN FC

Founded: 1924
Former Name(s): None
Nickname: The Ports
Ground: Shamrock Park, Brownstown Road, Portadown, Co. Armagh.
Record Attendance: 16,500 (1962)
Colours: Shirts - Red
         Shorts - Red
Phone No.: (01762) 332726

Pitch Size: 110 x 60 yds
Ground Capacity: 15,000
Seating Capacity: 2,700
Correspondence Address: M. Foster, The Cottage, Cabragh, Tandragee, Co. Armagh
Contact No.: (01762) 841566 (Home)

GENERAL INFORMATION
Supporters Club Administrator: M. Foster
Address: c/o Club
Telephone Number: (01762) 841566
Car Parking: At Ground (200 Cars)
Coach Parking: At Ground
Nearest Railway Station: Portadown (0.3 mile)
Nearest Bus Station: Fair Green, Portadown (0.5 mile)
Club Shop: Yes
Opening Times: Matchdays only
Telephone No.: (01762) 332726
Postal Sales: Yes
Nearest Police Station: Portadown (1 mile)
Police Force: RUC
Police Telephone No.: (01762) 332424

DISABLED SUPPORTERS INFORMATION
Wheelchairs: Accommodated
Disabled Toilets: Yes
The Blind: No Special Facilities

ADMISSION INFO (1996/97 PRICES)
Adult Standing: £4.00
Adult Seating: £5.00
Child Standing: £3.00
Child Seating: £3.00
Concessionary Standing: £3.00
Concessionary Seating: £3.00
Programme Price: £1.00
FAX Number: None

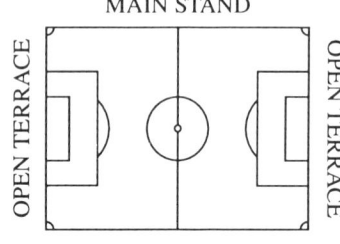

Travelling Supporters Information:
Routes: Exit M1 at junction 11 & take M12 to Portadown. In town centre turn left at St. John's Church into Armagh Road. Pass over bridge and turn right into Browns town road just before traffic lights for ground.

ARMAGH CITY FC

Founded: 1964
Former Name(s): Milford Everton FC
Nickname: None
Ground: Home Park, 41A Ballynahonemore Rd., Ardmore, Newry Rd., Armagh, BT60 1JD
Record Attendance: 300
Colours: Shirts - Azure & Black Stripes
   Shorts - Black

Contact No.: (01861) 526151
Pitch Size: 112 x 70 yds
Ground Capacity: 3,000
Seating Capacity: None
Correspondence Address:
A. Murphy, 4 Sperrin Park, BT61 9EP

GENERAL INFORMATION
Supporters Club Administrator: None
Address: –
Telephone Number: –
Car Parking: At Ground
Coach Parking: At Ground
Nearest Railway Station: Portadown (11 miles)
Nearest Bus Station: Armagh (1.5 miles)
Club Shop: None
Opening Times: –
Telephone No.: –
Postal Sales: –
Nearest Police Station: Armagh
Police Force: RUC
Police Telephone No.: (01861) 523311

DISABLED SUPPORTERS INFORMATION
Wheelchairs: Accommodated
Disabled Toilets: Yes
The Blind: No Special Facilities

ADMISSION INFO (1996/97 PRICES)
Adult Standing: £2.00
Child Standing: Free
Concessionary Standing: £1.00
Programme Price: 50p
FAX Number: None

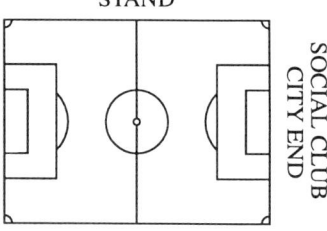

Travelling Supporters Information:
Routes: Take the A3 or the A28 into the centre of Armagh. At the junction of the A3 & A28 turn off past RUC station and continue along for about 1 mile. After going down a steep hill turn left into road signposted Ardmore and continue for 0.5 mile. Ground is at the bottom of road on the left.

BALLINAMALLARD UNITED FC

Founded: 1975
Former Name(s): None
Nickname: 'Mallards' or 'Blues'
Ground: Ferney Park, Ballinamallard, Co. Fermanagh
Record Attendance: 1,020 (vs Cliftonville 1994/95)
Colours: Shirts - Sky Blue
            Shorts - White

Contact No.: (01365) 388600
Pitch Size: 110 x 70yds
Ground Capacity: 4,000
Seating Capacity: 250
Correspondence Address: c/o Club

GENERAL INFORMATION
Supporters Club Administrator: The Secretary
Address: c/o Club
Telephone Number: (01365) 388600
Car Parking: At Ground (50 cars)
Coach Parking: At Ground
Nearest Railway Station: None nearby
Nearest Bus Station: Ballinamllard 0.5 mile
Club Shop: Social Club
Opening Times: 8.00 pm-11.30pm Tuesday to Sunday
Telephone No.: (01365) 388600
Postal Sales: No
Nearest Police Station: Ballinamallard
Police Force: RUC
Police Telephone No.: (01365) 322823

DISABLED SUPPORTERS INFORMATION
Wheelchairs: Accommodated
Disabled Toilets: In Social Club
The Blind: No Special Facilities

ADMISSION INFO (1996/97 PRICES)
Adult Standing: £3.00
Adult Seating: £3.00
Child Standing: Free
Child Seating: Free
Concessionary Standing: £3.00
Concessionary Seating: £3.00
Programme Price: 50p
FAX Number: None

SOCIAL CLUB

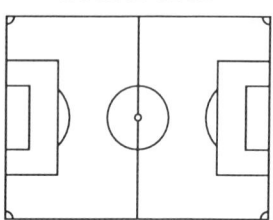

Travelling Supporters Information:
Routes: Ballinamallard is situated about 10 miles north off Enniskillen on the B46. The ground is 0.25 mile to the south of the village next door to Swiftsoft Computers.

BALLYMONEY UNITED FC

Founded: 1944
Former Name(s): Coronation Blues FC
Nickname: None
Ground: The Showgrounds, Ballymoney, Co. Antrim. Ground (012656) 65831
Phone No.: (012656) 65831
Record Attendance: Not known
Colours: Shirts - Red
  Shorts - White

Pitch Size: 110 x 72 yds
Ground Capacity: 5,000
Seating Capacity: 100
Correspondence Address: c/o O. Muldoon, 41 Margaret Ave, Ballymoney, B753 6BY
Contact No.: (012656) 66054

GENERAL INFORMATION
Supporters Club Administrator: None
Address: –
Telephone Number: –
Car Parking: At Ground
Coach Parking: At Ground
Nearest Railway Station: Ballymoney (0.25 mile)
Nearest Bus Station: Ballymoney (0.25mile)
Club Shop: None
Opening Times: –
Telephone No.: –
Postal Sales: –
Nearest Police Station: Ballmoney (adjacent)
Police Force: RUC
Police Telephone No.: (012656) 62222

DISABLED SUPPORTERS INFORMATION
Wheelchairs: Accommodated
Disabled Toilets: Yes
The Blind: No Special Facilities

ADMISSION INFO (1996/97 PRICES)
Adult Standing: £2.00
Adult Seating: £2.00
Child Standing: £1.00
Child Seating: £1.00
Concessionary Standing: £1.00
Concessionary Seating: £1.00
Programme Price: None
FAX Number: None

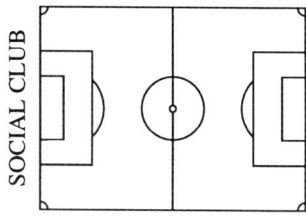

Travelling Supporters Information:
Routes: Take the B66 into the town centre. Pass church on left and ground is adjacent to new shopping centre on North Road.

BANBRIDGE TOWN FC

Founded: 1947
Former Name(s): None
Nickname: None
Ground: Crystal Park, Castlewellan Road, Banbridge, Co. Down.
Record Attendance: Not known
Colours: Shirts - Red & Black Stripes
Shorts - Black

Contact No.: (018206) 22081
Pitch Size: 112 x 72 yds
Ground Capacity: 1,500
Seating Capacity: None
Correspondence Address:
Norman Livingston, c/o Club

GENERAL INFORMATION
Supporters Club Administrator: None
Address: –
Telephone Number: –
Car Parking: Street Parking
Coach Parking: Street Parking
Nearest Railway Station: Portadown (10 miles)
Nearest Bus Station: Banbridge
Club Shop: None
Opening Times: –
Telephone No.: –
Postal Sales: –
Nearest Police Station: Banbridge
Police Force: RUC
Police Telephone No.: (018206) 62222

DISABLED SUPPORTERS INFORMATION
Wheelchairs: Accommodated
Disabled Toilets: None
The Blind: No Special Facilities

ADMISSION INFO (1996/97 PRICES)
Adult Standing: £3.00
Child Standing: £1.00
Concessionary Standing: £1.00
Programme Price: None
FAX Number: None

SOCIAL CLUB

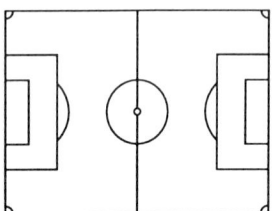

Travelling Supporters Information:
Routes: Exit the A1 onto the A50 for Banbridge. In the town centre, pass RUC station then turn left just before labour exchange and ground is immediately on left.

BRANTWOOD FC

Founded: 1903
Former Name(s): None
Nickname: Brants
Ground: Skegoneill Park, Skegoneill Ave, Belfast 15.
Record Attendance: Not known
Colours: Shirts - Royal Blue
  Shorts - White
Phone No.: (01232) 772370

Pitch Size: 108 x 72 yds
Ground Capacity: 4,000
Seating Capacity: None
Correspondence Address: David Holmes, 9c Bank Parade, Belfast 15
Contact No.: (01232) 771153

GENERAL INFORMATION
Supporters Club Administrator: None
Address: –
Telephone Number: –
Car Parking: At Ground
Coach Parking: At Ground
Nearest Railway Station: Belfast
Nearest Bus Station: Belfast
Club Shop: None
Opening Times: –
Telephone No.: –
Postal Sales: –
Nearest Police Station: Lisburn Road
Police Force: RUC
Police Telephone No.: (01232) 650222

DISABLED SUPPORTERS INFORMATION
Wheelchairs: Accommodated
Disabled Toilets: None
The Blind: No Special Facilities

ADMISSION INFO (1996/97 PRICES)
Adult Standing: £1.75
Child Standing: 75p
Concessionary Standing: 75p
Programme Price: None
FAX Number: None

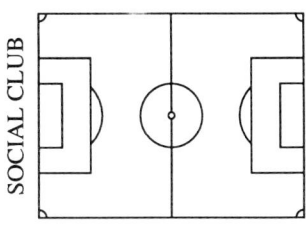

Travelling Supporters Information:
Routes: Exit M2 at junction 1 and take the Shore Road southwards. Just before the Grove playing fields, turn right into Skegoneill Ave and ground is on the right at junction with Jellicoe Ave.

CHIMNEY CORNER FC

Founded: 1952
Former Name(s): None
Nickname: None
Ground: Allen Park, Antrim, Co. Antrim
Phone No.: (01849) 461256
Record Attendance: 600
Colours: Shirts - Red
Shorts - Black

Pitch Size: 114 x 76 yds
Ground Capacity: 2,000
Seating Capacity: None
Correspondence Address: J Stewart, 48 Grant Avenue, Randalstown, Co. Antrim
Contact No.: (01849) 479544/472188

GENERAL INFORMATION
Supporters Club Administrator: Mel Campbell
Address: As above
Telephone Number: (01849) 472188
Car Parking: At Ground
Coach Parking: At Ground
Nearest Railway Station: Antrim
Nearest Bus Station: Antrim
Club Shop: At Bar
Opening Times: Monday to Sunday
Telephone No.: (01849) 461256
Postal Sales: No
Nearest Police Station: Antrim
Police Force: RUC
Police Telephone No.: (01849) 47222

DISABLED SUPPORTERS INFORMATION
Wheelchairs: Accommodated
Disabled Toilets: Yes
The Blind: No Special Facilities

ADMISSION INFO (1996/97 PRICES)
Adult Standing: £2.00
Child Standing: £1.00
Concessionary Standing: £1.00
Programme Price: 50p
FAX Number: None

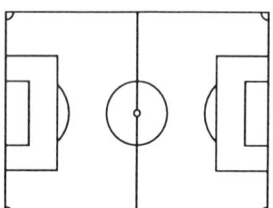
STAND

Travelling Supporters Information:
Routes: Take the A6 to Antrim town centre. Turn right at traffic lights by RUC station then turn left at roundabout into Randals town Road. Continue for about 1 mile and ground is on the right after the Rugby Ground.

COOKSTOWN UNITED FC

Founded: 1976
Former Name(s): None
Nickname: None
Ground: Millbank Park, Drapersfield, Cookstown, Co. Tyrone.
Phone No.: (016487) 64286
Record Attendance: Not known
Colours: Shirts - Royal Blue
　　　　　Shorts - White

Pitch Size: 112 x 72 yds
Ground Capacity: 1,500
Seating Capacity: 24
Correspondence Address: W. Jordan, 7 Highfield Road, Magherafelt, BT45 5 JD
Contact No.: (01648) 34159

GENERAL INFORMATION
Supporters Club Administrator: None
Address: –
Telephone Number: –
Car Parking: At Ground
Coach Parking: At Ground
Nearest Railway Station: Portadown (35 miles)
Nearest Bus Station: Cookstown
Club Shop: None
Opening Times: –
Telephone No.: –
Postal Sales: –
Nearest Police Station: Cookstown
Police Force: RUC
Police Telephone No.: –

DISABLED SUPPORTERS INFORMATION
Wheelchairs: Accommodated
Disabled Toilets: None
The Blind: No Special Facilities

ADMISSION INFO (1996/97 PRICES)
Adult Standing: £2.00
Adult Seating: £2.00
Child Standing: £1.00
Child Seating: £1.00
Concessionary Standing: £1.00
Concessionary Seating: £1.00
Programme Price: None
FAX Number: None

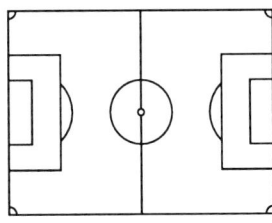

SOCIAL CLUB

Travelling Supporters Information:
Routes: Take the A29 to Cookstown and turn at mini-roundabout towards leisure centre. After 1 mile turn right (signposted Drapersfield) and follow road to Drapersfield. Ground is on the right adjacent to nursing home.

DUNDELA FC

Founded: 1895
Former Name(s): None
Nickname: Henrun
Ground: Wilgar Park, Strandtown, Belfast.
Phone No.: (01232) 655955
Record Attendance: Not known
Colours: Shirts - Green
Shorts - White

Pitch Size: 100 x 60 yds
Ground Capacity: 3,500
Seating Capacity: 40
Correspondence Address: G Sterling, 16 Lisavon Street, Belfast BT4 1LH
Contact No.: (01232) 652885

GENERAL INFORMATION
Supporters Club Administrator: None
Address: –
Telephone Number: –
Car Parking: At Ground
Coach Parking: At Ground
Nearest Railway Station: Belfast
Nearest Bus Station: –
Club Shop: None
Opening Times: –
Telephone No.: –
Postal Sales: –
Nearest Police Station: Strandtown
Police Force: RUC
Police Telephone No.: (01232) 650222

DISABLED SUPPORTERS INFORMATION
Wheelchairs: Not Accommodated
Disabled Toilets: None
The Blind: No Special Facilities

ADMISSION INFO (1996/97 PRICES)
Adult Standing: £2.00
Adult Seating: £2.00
Child Standing: £1.60
Child Seating: £1.00
Concessionary Standing: £1.00
Concessionary Seating: £1.00
Programme Price: None
FAX Number: None

SOCIAL CLUB STAND

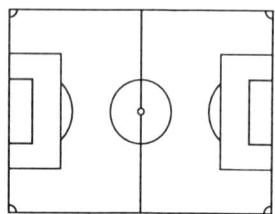

OPEN TERRACING

Travelling Supporters Information:
Routes: Exit M3 at junction with A2 and follow signs for A20 into Newtownards Road. Turn left at main junction into Hollywood Road. Pass RUC station and turn right into Dundela Avenue. Ground is on left at junction with Dundela Crescent.

DUNGANNON SWIFTS FC

Founded: 1949
Former Name(s): None
Nickname: Swifts
Ground: Stangmore Park, Dungannon, Co. Tyrone
Record Attendance: 4,876
Colours: Shirts - Royal Blue/White Trim
   Shorts - Royal Blue/White Trim
Contact No.: (01868) 723257

Pitch Size: 112 x 70 yds
Ground Capacity: 5,000
Seating Capacity: 270
Correspondence Address: David Gallagher, 15 Hillcrest Park, Moygashel, Dungannon, BT71 7RH

GENERAL INFORMATION
Supporters Club Administrator: Kenny Archer
Address: c/o Club
Telephone Number: (01868) 722271
Car Parking: At Ground
Coach Parking: At Ground
Nearest Railway Station: Portadown 12mls
Nearest Bus Station: Dungannon 1 ml
Club Shop: No
Opening Times: –
Telephone No.: –
Postal Sales: No
Nearest Police Station: Dungannon
Police Force: RUC
Police Telephone No.: (01868) 752525

DISABLED SUPPORTERS INFORMATION
Wheelchairs: Accommodated
Disabled Toilets: None
The Blind: No Special Facilities

ADMISSION INFO (1996/97 PRICES)
Adult Standing: £3.00
Adult Seating: £3.00
Child Standing: £1.50
Child Seating: £1.50
Concessionary Standing: £1.50
Concessionary Seating: £1.50
Programme Price: 50p
FAX Number: None

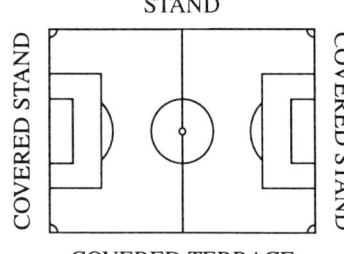

Travelling Supporters Information:
Routes: Take the M1 to junction 15, then the A29 towards Dungannon. Ground is situated on the outskirts of the town on the right-hand side of the A29 just before the Rugby Ground.

HARLAND & WOLFF WELDERS FC

Founded: 1965
Former Name(s): None
Nickname: None
Ground: Tillysburn Park, Hollywood Road, Belfast BT4.
Record Attendance: Not known
Colours: Shirts - Amber
　　　　 Shorts - Black
Phone No.: (01232) 761214

Pitch Size: 110 x 80 yds
Ground Capacity: Approximately 1,500
Seating Capacity: None
Correspondence Address: F. Magee, 68 Organe Field Avenue, Belfast BT5 6DH
Contact No.: (01232) 672210

GENERAL INFORMATION
Supporters Club Administrator: None
Address: –
Telephone Number: –
Car Parking: At Ground
Coach Parking: At Ground
Nearest Railway Station: Botanic Station, 2 miles
Nearest Bus Station: Belfast
Club Shop: None
Opening Times: –
Telephone No.: –
Postal Sales: –
Nearest Police Station: Strandtown
Police Force: RUC
Police Telephone No.: (01232) 650222

DISABLED SUPPORTERS INFORMATION
Wheelchairs: Accommodated
Disabled Toilets: None
The Blind: No Special Facilities

ADMISSION INFO (1996/97 PRICES)
Adult Standing: £1.50
Child Standing: 40p
Concessionary Standing: 40p
Programme Price: None
FAX Number: None

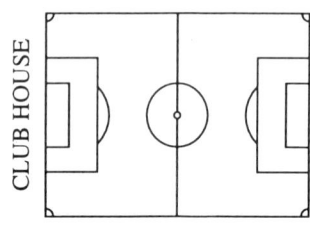

Travelling Supporters Information:
Routes: The Ground is situated next to the airport. Take the A2 bypass to the junction with the A504 (Hollywood Road) and ground is on the right next to the aircraft park.

INSTITUTE FC

Founded: –
Former Name(s): None
Nickname: 'Stute'
Ground: YMCA Ground, Drumahoe, Londonderry
Record Attendance: Not known
Colours: Shirts - Sky Blue
   Shorts - Sky Blue

Contact No.: (01504) 311634
Pitch Size: 112 x 72 yds
Ground Capacity: 1,500
Seating Capacity: None
Correspondence Address: Paul Kee, 102 Spencer Road, Waterside, Londonderry BT47

GENERAL INFORMATION
Supporters Club Administrator: None
Address: –
Telephone Number: –
Car Parking: At Ground
Coach Parking: At Ground
Nearest Railway Station: Londonderry
Nearest Bus Station: Londonderry
Club Shop: None
Opening Times: –
Telephone No.: –
Postal Sales: –
Nearest Police Station: Waterside (3 miles)
Police Force: RUC
Police Telephone No.: (01504) 766797

DISABLED SUPPORTERS INFORMATION
Wheelchairs: Accommodated
Disabled Toilets: None
The Blind: No Special Facilities

ADMISSION INFO (1996/97 PRICES)
Adult Standing: No charges normally
Child Standing: No charges normally
Concessionary Standing: No charges normally
Programme Price: None
FAX Number: (01504) 311634

YMCA BUILDING

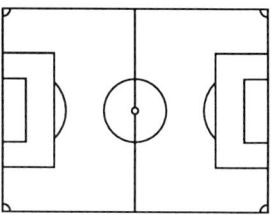

Travelling Supporters Information:
Routes: The ground is situated at Drumahoe, a village 3 miles from the centre of Londonderry on the Waterside side of the River Foyle. Take the main Belfast road and ground is on the right opposite Faughan Valley High School.

LIMAVADY UNITED FC

Founded: 1876
Former Name(s): None
Nickname: United
Ground: The Showgrounds, Rathmore Road, Limavady, Co. Londonderry
Record Attendance: Not known
Colours: Shirts - Royal Blue
  Shorts - White

Contact No.: (015047) 25311
Pitch Size: 100 x 80 yds
Ground Capacity: 1,000
Seating Capacity: None
Correspondence Address: c/o Club

GENERAL INFORMATION
Supporters Club Administrator: None
Address: -
Telephone Number: -
Car Parking: At Ground
Coach Parking: At Ground
Nearest Railway Station: Londonderry
Nearest Bus Station: Limavady
Club Shop: None
Opening Times: –
Telephone No.: –
Postal Sales: –
Nearest Police Station: Limavady
Police Force: RUC
Police Telephone No.: (015047) 66797

DISABLED SUPPORTERS INFORMATION
Wheelchairs: Accommodated
Disabled Toilets: None
The Blind: No Special Facilities

ADMISSION INFO (1996/97 PRICES)
Adult Standing: £2.00
Child Standing: N/C
Concessionary Standing: £2.00
Programme Price: None
FAX Number: None

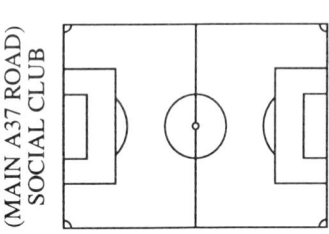

Travelling Supporters Information:
Routes: Take the A37 to Limavady and ground is situated on the main road 0.5 mile from the Town Centre on east (Coleraine) side of town.

LOUGHGALL FC

Founded: 1967
Former Name(s): None
Nickname: None
Ground: Lakeview Park, Loughgall, Co. Armagh
Record Attendance: None Known
Colours: Shirts - Blue & White
　　　　　Shorts - Blue
Phone No.: (01762) 891400

Pitch Size: 110 x 72 Yds
Ground Capacity: 1,500
Seating Capacity: 74
Correspondence Address: Noel McClure, 33 Ardmore Drive, Armagh, BT60 1JB
Contact No.: (01861) 526768

GENERAL INFORMATION
Supporters Club Administrator: None
Address: –
Telephone Number: –
Car Parking: At Ground
Coach Parking: At Ground
Nearest Railway Station: Portadown (5 miles)
Nearest Bus Station: Portadown (5 miles)
Club Shop: Yes
Opening Times: Matchdays
Telephone No.: (01762) 891400
Postal Sales: Yes
Nearest Police Station: Loughgall
Police Force: RUC
Police Telephone No.: (01861) 523311

DISABLED SUPPORTERS INFORMATION
Wheelchairs: Accommodated
Disabled Toilets: None
The Blind: No Special Facilities

ADMISSION INFO (1996/97 PRICES)
Adult Standing: £3.00
Child Standing: £1.50
Concessionary Standing: £1.50
Programme Price: None
FAX Number: None

SOCIAL CLUB

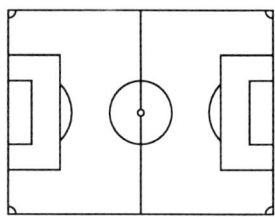

Travelling Supporters Information:
Routes: Loughgall is situated on the B77 midway between Armagh and Portadown. Ground is opposite RUC station in village centre.

MOYOLA PARK FC

Founded: 1880
Former Name(s): None
Nickname: The Park
Ground: Moyola Park, Castledawson, Co. Londonderry
Record Attendance: 400
Colours: Shirts - Royal Blue
　　　　　　Shorts - White
Contact No.: (01648) 468728

Pitch Size: 110 x 65 yds
Ground Capacity: 2000
Seating Capacity: None
Correspondence Address: c/o 7 Bridge Street Castledawson, Magherafelt, Co. Londonderry, BT45 8AD
Social Club Address: 16 Main Street, Castledawson, Magherafelt, Co. Londonderry
Tel: (01648) 468745

GENERAL INFORMATION
Supporters Club Administrator: Billy Lennox
Address: 44 Annaghmore Road, Castledowson, Co. Londonderry
Telephone Number: (01648) 468363
Car Parking: At Ground
Coach Parking: Bridge street
Nearest Railway Station: Antrim (15 miles)
Nearest Bus Station: Magherafelt (3 miles)
Club Shop: None
Opening Times: –
Telephone No.: –
Postal Sales: –
Nearest Police Station: Castledawson (0.5 mile)
Police Force: RUC
Police Telephone No.: (01648) 68205/33701

DISABLED SUPPORTERS INFORMATION
Wheelchairs: Accommodated
Disabled Toilets: Yes
The Blind: No Special Facilities

ADMISSION INFO (1996/97 PRICES)
Adult Standing: £2-00
Child Standing: £1-00
Concessionary Standing: £1-00
Programme Price: None
FAX Number: (01648) 469476

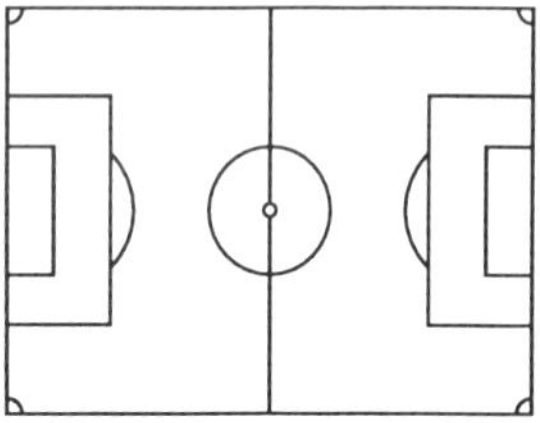

```
         AVENUE SIDE
     ┌─────────────────┐
  C  │    │       │    │  C
  A  │    │       │    │  H
  S  │    │   ○   │    │  R
  T  │    │       │    │  I
  L  │    │       │    │  S
  E  │    │       │    │  T
     │    │       │    │  C
  E  │    │       │    │  H
  N  │    │       │    │  U
  D  │    │       │    │  R
     │    │       │    │  C
     │    │       │    │  H
     └─────────────────┘   E
        PAVILION SIDE      N
                           D
```

Travelling Supporters Information:
Routes: Castledawson is situated 1 mile north-east of the A6 on the A54. Ground is in Bridge Street down lane beside church.

ROYAL ULSTER CONSTABULARY FC

Founded: 1956
Former Name(s): None
Nickname: 'Police'
Ground: Newforge Lane, Belfast, BT9 5NN
Record Attendance: Not known
Colours: Shirts - Green & Black Stripes
　　　　　Shorts - Black
Contact No.: (01232) 681027

Pitch Size: 110x 70 yds
Ground Capacity: Not specified
Seating Capacity: None
Correspondence Address: Central Process Office, Strandtown RUC Station, Belfast BT04 3BQ

GENERAL INFORMATION
Supporters Club Administrator: None
Address: –
Telephone Number: –
Car Parking: At Ground
Coach Parking: At Ground
Nearest Railway Station: Belfast Central
Nearest Bus Station: Victoria Street
Club Shop: None
Opening Times: –
Telephone No.: –
Postal Sales: –
Nearest Police Station: Lisburn Road
Police Force: RUC
Police Telephone No.: (01232) 650222

DISABLED SUPPORTERS INFORMATION
Wheelchairs: Accommodated
Disabled Toilets: None
The Blind: No Special Facilities

ADMISSION INFO (1996/97 PRICES)
Adult Standing: No Charge
Child Standing: No Charge
Concessionary Standing: No Charge
Programme Price: 50p
FAX Number: (01232) 259781

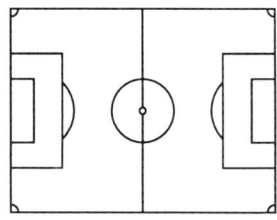

Travelling Supporters Information:
Routes: From City Centre: Take University Road – Malone Road to Newforge Lane

TOBERMORE UNITED FC

Founded: 1965
Former Name(s): None
Nickname: None
Ground: Fortwilliam Park, Maghera Road, Tobermore, Co. Londonderry
Record Attendance: Not known
Colours: Shirts - Red
　　　　　Shorts - Black
Phone No.: (01648) 43714

Pitch Size: 112 x 73 yds
Ground Capacity: 1,500
Seating Capacity: None
Correspondence Address: Tom Cassidy, 8 Desertmartin Road, Tobermore, Magherafelt, BT45 5QY
Contact No.: (01648) 43352 (Home); (01648) 42425 (Business)

GENERAL INFORMATION
Supporters Club Administrator: None
Address: –
Telephone Number: –
Car Parking: At Ground
Coach Parking: At Ground
Nearest Railway Station: Antrim (20 miles)
Nearest Bus Station: Magherafelt
Club Shop: None
Opening Times: –
Telephone No.: –
Postal Sales: –
Nearest Police Station: Maghera
Police Force: RUC
Police Telephone No.: (01504) 367337

DISABLED SUPPORTERS INFORMATION
Wheelchairs: Accommodated
Disabled Toilets: None
The Blind: No Special Facilities

ADMISSION INFO (1996/97 PRICES)
Adult Standing: £2.00
Child Standing: £1.00
Concessionary Standing: £1.00
Programme Price: None
FAX Number: None

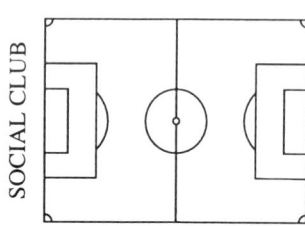

Travelling Supporters Information:
Routes: Tobermore is situated south of the A6 on the A29. Ground is 0.5 mile south of village on left-hand side of road.

STATISTICS SEASON 1995-96

Contents:

Smirnoff Premier League
Home & Away Chart
Final Table

Smirnoff 1st Division
Home & Away Chart
Final Table

Wilkinson Sword Irish League 'B' Division Section One
Final Table

Smirnoff Premier League 1995/96 Season	Ards	Bangor	Cliftonville	Crusaders	Glenavon	Glentoran	Linfield	Portadown
Ards	■	3-0	3-0	0-0	1-1	1-4	2-3	1-1
	■	2-1	2-2	0-1	1-2	0-2	1-2	0-2
Bangor	2-1	■	3-2	1-2	0-1	1-6	1-2	0-3
	0-1	■	2-3	0-2	1-2	1-1	0-2	0-0
Cliftonville	0-0	2-1	■	1-4	2-2	0-0	1-1	0-3
	1-0	1-1	■	2-1	0-1	1-0	0-0	0-4
Crusaders	1-2	2-0	1-0	■	1-2	2-1	3-0	3-1
	2-0	1-0	1-1	■	1-0	1-3	4-2	3-3
Glenavon	3-0	1-0	1-2	4-0	■	2-3	0-3	0-1
	3-1	0-1	1-1	1-1	■	1-3	2-2	7-0
Glentoran	3-2	1-1	1-1	3-1	0-2	■	0-3	1-1
	3-1	3-0	2-1	2-2	1-2	■	3-0	3-3
Linfield	0-0	0-0	0-0	1-2	0-3	0-4	■	1-0
	0-0	2-1	3-1	0-1	2-1	2-0	■	0-1
Portadown	3-1	4-2	6-1	1-1	2-1	3-1	3-2	■
	1-3	4-3	4-1	1-1	2-1	3-2	1-1	■

SMIRNOFF PREMIER LEAGUE 1995/96
LEAGUE TABLE FINAL

Portadown	28	16	8	4	61	40	56
Crusaders	28	15	7	6	45	32	52
Glentoran	28	13	7	8	56	38	46
Glenavon	28	13	5	10	47	32	44
Linfield	28	11	8	9	34	35	41
Cliftonville	28	6	11	11	27	48	29
Ards	28	6	7	15	29	43	25
Bangor	28	3	5	20	23	54	14

Champions : - Portadown
Relegated : - Bangor

Smirnoff First Division 1995/96 Season	Ballyclare Comrades	Ballymena United	Carrick Rangers	Coleraine	Distillery	Larne	Newry Town	Omagh Town
Ballyclare Comrades		1-3	2-1	1-0	0-2	2-3	1-1	1-2
		0-1	3-2	0-2	0-3	1-1	3-2	0-5
Ballymena United	0-0		3-1	1-2	0-1	0-0	0-0	2-0
	2-1		1-2	4-3	1-1	2-2	3-0	2-0
Carrick Rangers	3-0	1-1		0-3	0-0	1-0	3-1	2-3
	0-3	0-2		2-5	0-0	1-0	1-0	2-0
Coleraine	2-0	1-1	6-0		2-1	1-0	8-0	5-2
	1-3	4-0	5-1		4-2	3-2	5-0	2-1
Distillery	1-2	0-1	3-1	1-1		1-0	2-1	3-2
	0-1	1-3	2-1	1-1		0-1	1-1	0-1
Larne	2-0	0-0	0-1	0-2	2-0		1-2	2-2
	0-1	0-1	3-1	1-2	3-1		1-1	1-3
Newry Town	2-0	1-2	2-3	1-4	2-5	3-2		1-2
	3-0	1-0	1-0	1-2	0-2	2-0		2-2
Omagh Town	1-3	0-0	1-0	2-2	3-1	1-3	1-0	
	3-0	2-2	6-2	0-4	0-0	1-1	4-0	

SMIRNOFF 1ST DIVISION 1995/96
LEAGUE TABLE FINAL

Coleraine	28	21	4	3	82	28	67
Ballymena United	28	13	10	5	38	25	49
Omagh Town	28	12	7	9	50	43	43
Distillery	28	10	7	11	35	34	37
Ballyclare Coms.	28	10	3	15	29	48	33
Carrick Rangers	28	9	3	16	32	56	30
Larne	28	7	7	14	31	36	28
Newry Town	28	7	5	16	31	58	26

Promoted : - Coleraine

WILKINSON SWORD IRISH LEAGUE
'B' DIVISION SECTION 1 1995/96 SEASON
LEAGUE TABLE FINAL

Loughgall	30	24	4	2	58	23	76
Dungannon Swifts	30	21	5	4	91	32	68
Banbridge Town	30	21	4	5	78	28	67
Dundela	30	18	5	7	80	35	59
Limavady United	30	17	7	6	71	38	58
Harland & Wolff Welds.	30	17	6	7	71	39	57
Chimney Corner	30	16	7	7	70	36	55
R.U.C.	30	13	4	13	54	41	43
Ballinamallard United	30	10	7	13	50	51	37
Armagh City	30	10	5	15	46	64	35
Tobermore United	30	8	4	18	36	79	28
Moyola Park	30	6	6	18	45	72	24
Brantwood	30	5	7	18	32	70	22
Ballymoney United	30	5	5	20	33	74	20
Cookstown United	30	5	5	20	24	78	20
Queen's University	30	1	5	24	20	98	8 *

Champions : - Loughgall

* Queen's University was not re-elected by the Irish League for next season.
Institute F.C. from Londonderry will replace Queen's for the 1996/97 Season.

NORTHERN IRELAND INTERNATIONAL LINE-UPS AND STATISTICS 1995

29th March 1995
v REPUBLIC OF IRELAND (ECQ)
Dublin
Fettis   Hull City
Patterson   Crystal Palace
Worthington   Leeds United
Taggart   Barnsley
McDonald   Q.P.R.
Morrow   Arsenal
Gillespie   Newcastle United
Magilton   Southampton
Dowie   Crystal Palace
Hill   Leicester City
Hughes   Strasbourg
Result 1-1 Dowie

26th April 1995
v LATVIA (ECQ) *Riga*
Fettis   Hull City
Patterson   Crystal Palace
Worthington   Leeds United
Hunter   Wrexham
McDonald   Q.P.R.
Hill   Leicester City
Gillespie   Newcastle Utd. (sub. O'Boyle)
Wilson   Walsall
Dowie   Crystal Palace (sub. Quinn)
Horlock   Swindon Town
Hughes   Strasbourg
Result 1-0 Dowie (pen)

22nd May 1995
v CANADA *Edmonton*
Fettis   Hull City
Patterson   Crystal Palace
Rowland   West Ham United
Taggart   Barnsley
McDonald   Q.P.R. (sub. McGibbon)
Horlock   Swindon Tn. (sub. Worthington)
Gillespie   Newcastle Utd (sub. McMahon)
Magilton   Southampton
Gray   Sunderland
Dowie   Crystal Palace (sub. O'Boyle)
Hughes   Strasbourg
Result 0-2

25th May 1995
v CHILE *Edmonton*
Fettis   Hull City
McGibbon   Manchester U. (sub. Patterson)
Worthington   Leeds United
Taggart   Barnsley
McDonald   Q.P.R.
Rowland   West Ham United
McMahon   Tott'm. Hotspur (sub. Gillespie)
Magilton   Southampton (sub. O'Boyle)
Lennon   Crewe Alexandra
Dowie   Crystal Palace (sub. Gray)
Hughes   Strasbourg
Result 1-2 Dowie

7th June 1995
v LATVIA (ECQ) *Belfast*
Fettis   Hull City
McGibbon   Manchester U. (sub. Patterson)
Worthington   Leeds United
Taggart   Barnsley
McDonald   Q.P.R.
Morrow   Arsenal
McMahon   Tottenham Hotspur
Magilton   Southampton
Dowie   Crystal Palace
Rowland   West Ham Utd. (sub. Gillespie)
Hughes   Strasbourg
Result 1-2 Dowie

3rd September 1995
v PORTUGAL (ECQ) *Porto*
Fettis   Hull City
Morrow   Arsenal
Worthington   Leeds United
Hill   Leicester City
Hunter   Wrexham
Lomas   Manchester City
Gillespie   Newcastle United
Magilton   Southampton
Dowie   Crystal Palace (sub. Gray)
Lennon   Crewe Alexandra
Hughes   Strasbourg
Result 1-1 Hughes

NORTHERN IRELAND INTERNATIONAL LINE-UPS AND STATISTICS 1995-96

11th October 1995
v LIECHTENSTEIN (ECQ) *Eschen*
Fettis	Hull City (sub. Wood)
Lomas	Manchester City
Worthington	Leeds United
Hill	Leicester City
Hunter	Wrexham
Lennon	Crewe Alexandra
McMahon	Tott'm Hotspur (sub. McGibbon)
O'Neill	Hibernian
Quinn	Reading
Gray	Sunderland
Hughes	Strasbourg (sub. Rowland)

Result 4-0 O'Neill, McMahon, Quinn, Gray

15th November 1995
v AUSTRIA (ECQ) *Belfast*
Fettis	Hull City
Lomas	Manchester City
Worthington	Leeds United
Hunter	Wrexham
Hill	Leicester City
Lennon	Crewe Alexandra
Gillespie	Newcastle United
O'Neill	Hibernian
Dowie	West Ham United (sub. Quinn)
Gray	Sunderland (sub. McDonald)
Hughes	Strasbourg

Result 5-3 O'Neill 2, Dowie (pen), Hunter, Gray

27th March 1996
v NORWAY *Belfast*
Fettis	Nottingham Forest
Lomas	Manchester City
Worthington	Leeds United (sub. Rowland)
Hill	Leicester City
McDonald	Q.P.R.
Lennon	Leicester City
Gillespie	Newcastle United
O'Neill	Hibernian (sub. McMahon)
Dowie	West Ham United
Magilton	Southampton (sub. Patterson)
Hughes	West Ham United

Result 0-2

24th April 1996
v SWEDEN *Belfast*
Davison	Bolton Wanderers
Patterson	Luton Town
Worthington	Leeds United (sub. Quinn)
Hill	Leicester City
Hunter	Wrexham
Morrow	Arsenal
McCarthy	Port Vale
Lomas	Manchester City
McMahon	Tottenham Hotspur
O'Neill	Hibernian (sub. O'Boyle)
Rowland	West Ham United

Result 1-2 McMahon

29th May 1996
v GERMANY *Belfast*
Fettis	Nottingham Forest
Griffin	St. Johnstone
Worthington	Leeds United (sub. Rowland)
Hill	Leicester City
Hunter	Wrexham
Gillespie	Newcastle Utd. (sub. O'Boyle)
Lomas	Manchester City
Magilton	Southampton
McMahon	Tottenham Hotspur
Hughes	West Ham United
Dowie	West Ham United

Result 1-1 O'Boyle

FOOTBALL ASSOCIATION OF IRELAND

Founded
1921

Harp Lager National League
80 Merrion Square
Dublin 2
Republic of Ireland

Phone (00353) 1 – 6614181
Fax (00353) 1 – 6610931

Contents
Harp Lager Premier Division Clubs
Harp Lager 1st Division Clubs

BOHEMIAN FC

Founded: 1890
Former Name(s): None
Nickname: 'Gypsies'
Ground: Dalymount Park, Phibsborough, Dublin 7, Republic of Ireland
Ground No.: (01) 8680923/8682880
Record Attendance: 46,700
Colours: Shirts - Red & Black Stripes Shorts - Black

Contact No.: (01) 8480387 (Home); (088) 564119 (Mobile)
Pitch Size: 120x75 yds
Ground Capacity: 18,000
Seating Capacity: 1,800
Correspondence Address: c/o Donal Crowther, 44 Woodbine Drive, Raheny, Dublin 5, Republic of Ireland

GENERAL INFORMATION
Supporters Club Administrator: Greg Molloy
Address: c/o Club
Telephone Number: (01) 2842927 (Home), (01) 2989867 (Business)
Car Parking: Street Parking
Coach Parking: Street Parking
Nearest Railway Station: Connolly
Nearest Bus Station: Busaras
Club Shop: Yes
Opening Times: Matchdays only
Telephone No.: (01) 8680923
Postal Sales: Yes – Paddy Murray, c/o Club
Nearest Garda Station: Mountjoy, Dublin
Garda Telephone No.: (01) 8301720

DISABLED SUPPORTERS INFORMATION
Wheelchairs: Accommodated
Disabled Toilets: None
The Blind: No Special Facilities

ADMISSION INFO (1996/97 PRICES)
Adult Standing: £4.00
Adult Seating: £5.00
Child Standing: £2.00
Child Seating: £2.00
Concessionary Standing: On Application
Concessionary Seating:
Programme Price: £1.00
FAX Number: (01) 8681022

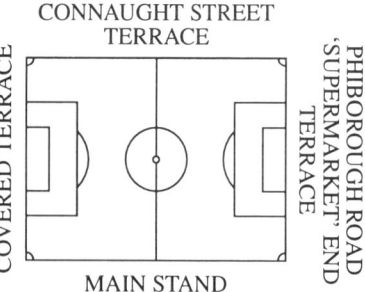

Travelling Supporters Information:
Routes: From The North (M1): M1 (becomes N1) Into Dublin, through Whitehall. Into right hand lane On Drumcondra Rd Lower, under railway bridge, right at the lights onto Whitworth Rd (just before Royal Canal). At top Whitworth Rd left onto Phibsborough Rd, stay in right hand lane for approx 250 metres, right at lights at Phibsboro Shopping Centre onto Connaught. St. Dalymount is immediately to your left; From the North (N2): N2 (becomes Finglas Rd) into Dublin through Finglas, past Glasnevin Cemetery (round tower on the left) after which traffic merges, stay right onto Prospect Rd, over Cross Guns Bridge (over railway and Royal Canal) onto Phibsborough Rd, then as per north (M1) above; From City Centre: North along O'Connell St (GPO on left) and at top go left onto Parnell Square West, onto Granby Row (National Wax Museum on right). Cross junction with Dorset St Upper onto St. Mary's Place, veer right at Black Church and right into Mountjoy Street. Cross junction with Blessington St onto Berkeley St (becomes Berkeley Rd) (Mater Hospital on right) and at end left at St. Peter's Church (immediately in front of you) onto New Cabra Rd and immediate right onto St Peter's Rd. Dalymount is immediately to your right; From West (N3): N3 (Navan Rd) into Dublin, keep left at Dalymount Park for Phibsborough and turn left at end of New Cabra Rd (St. Peter's Church on right) left onto St. Peter's Rd; From West (N4): N4 into Dublin, joining N7 at Con Colbert Rd. Cross major junction with South Circular Rd (SCR) onto St. John's Rd West (N7). Road veers left at Heuston Station to cross River Liffey, then right onto the city's North Quays heading East. Within 1,000 metres Wolfe Tone Quay becomes Ellis Quay becomes Arran Quay (church on left), next left onto Church St, becomes Constitution Hill, becomes Phibsborough Rd, through major crossroads with NCR and (after Philsboro Shopping centre on left) left onto Connaught St; From South West: N7 Naas Road into Inchicore, then follow instructions from West (Con Colbert Rd onwards).

BRAY WANDERERS FC

Founded: 1942
Former Name(s): None
Nickname: 'Seasiders'
Ground: Carlisle Ground, Bray, Co. Wicklow, Republic of Ireland
Ground No.: (01) 282814
Record Attendance: 3,000 (v Sligo Rovers)
Colours: Shirts - Green & White Stripes
　　　　　Shorts - White

Contact No.: (01) 2861685
Pitch Size: 113 x 70 yds
Ground Capacity: 3,000
Seating Capacity: None
Correspondence Address: c/o John O'Brien, 74 Newcourt Road, Bray, Co. Wicklow, Republic of Ireland

GENERAL INFORMATION
Supporters Club Administrator: None
Address: –
Telephone Number: –
Car Parking: Street Parking
Coach Parking: In Town
Nearest Railway Station: Bray (adjacent)
Nearest Bus Station: Bray
Club Shop: None
Opening Times: –
Telephone No.: –
Postal Sales: –
Nearest Garda Station: Bray (500 yds)
Garda Telephone No.: (01) 2862821

DISABLED SUPPORTERS INFORMATION
Wheelchairs: Accommodated
Disabled Toilets: None
The Blind: No Special Facilities

ADMISSION INFO (1996/97 PRICES)
Adult Standing: £4.00
Child Standing: £2.00
Concessionary Standing: £2.00
Programme Price: £1.00
FAX Number: None

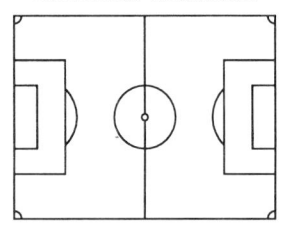

COVERED TERRACE

COVERED TERRACE

Travelling Supporters Information:
Routes: Take the N11/M11 to Bray. Ground is near the seafront next to the railway station.

CORK CITY FC

Founded: 1984
Former Name(s): None
Nickname: 'City'
Ground: Turners Cross Stadium, Curragh Road, Cork, Republic of Ireland
Record Attendance: 11,000 approximately
Colours: Shirts - White, Red Collar & Cuffs Shorts - Green
Contact No.: (021) 345588/342817

Pitch Size: 110 x 72yds
Ground Capacity: 12,000 approximately
Seating Capacity: None
Correspondence Address: Noel O'Mahony, Unit 10, University Hall Industial Park, Sarsfield Road, Wilton, Cork, Republic of Ireland

GENERAL INFORMATION
Supporters Club Administrator: Noelle Feeney
Address: 148 Pearse Road, Ballyphehane, Cork
Telephone Number: (021) 964055
Car Parking: Street Parking
Coach Parking: At Curragh Rd. Entrance
Nearest Railway Station: Kent Station, Cork
Nearest Bus Station: Parnell Place – No. 3 Bus from Patrick Street (Cash's Stores)
Club Shop: Yes
Opening Times: Matchdays
Telephone No.: No
Postal Sales: From Noelle Feeney
Nearest Garda Station: Anglesea Street
Garda Telephone No.: (021) 313031

DISABLED SUPPORTERS INFORMATION
Wheelchairs: on Side line
Disabled Toilets: None
The Blind: No Facilities

ADMISSION INFO (1996/97 PRICES)
Adult Standing: £4.00
Child Standing: £2.50 (Ages 4-10 £1.00)
Concessionary Standing: £2.50
Programme Price: £1.00
FAX Number: (021) 342824

BEAUFORT PARK
CURRAGH ROAD
END STAND & COVERED TERRACE
ST. ANNE'S PARK
DERRYNANE ROAD

Travelling Supporters Information:
Routes: From Dublin and East: Enter city on Lower Glanmire road, left onto Water St. at railway bridge (one-way system, follow 'City Centre' directions). Along quays, crossing at first bridge (Michael Collins) and straight on over south channel of river. Over next bridge (De Valera), on through Albert Street taking first right and immediate left onto South Link Road. Thereafter pass under pedestrian bridge and three flyovers, exiting immediate left after third onto South Douglas Road. Left turn here, straight ahead at mini-roundabout and left at traffic lights onto Curragh Road. Stadium 200m on right; From West: Entering on Carrigohane 'Straight' Road onto Western Road as far as University gates and left into one-way system passing 'Grand Central' amusement arcade on your right and behind the court house on Liberty Street until forced right turn (no other option!) onto South Main Street arriving at bridge with traffic lights (Beamish and Crawford Brewery on right). Cross bridge taking left at Kozy Korner pub. Faced with three direct routes at next junction choose centre, Evergreen Road (i.e. left of steep climb). Straight through traffic lights and right at second set. Stadium 200m on right; From North: Limerick etc follow signs for 'Blackpool'. Take first right after Blackpool fire station and immediate left onto Gerald Griffin Street. Straight through traffic lights at north Cathedral junction onto Shandon Street and across bridge at end taking sharp right, then first left and left again at traffic lights onto Adelaide Street and right onto North Main Street. Straight ahead into South Main Street and follow directions for Western entry from this point.

DERRY CITY FC

Founded: 1928
Former Name(s): None
Nickname: 'Candystripes'
Ground: Brandywell Stadium, Derry, Co. Londonderry, Northern Ireland.
Ground No.: (01504) 262276
Record Attendance: Not known
Colours: Shirts - Purple
 Shorts - Black

Contact No.: (01504) 374542
Pitch Size: 108 x 72 yds
Ground Capacity: 8,500
Seating Capacity: 3,000
Correspondence Address: c/o 12 Queen Street, Derry, BT48 7EG

GENERAL INFORMATION
Supporters Club Administrator: None
Address: –
Telephone Number: –
Car Parking: Street parking
Coach Parking: At ground
Nearest Railway Station: Waterside (1 mile)
Nearest Bus Station: Waterside (1mile)
Club Shop: None
Opening Times: –
Telephone No.: –
Postal Sales: –
Nearest Police Station: Waterside (1 mile)
Police Force: RUC
Police Telephone No.: (01504) 766797

DISABLED SUPPORTERS INFORMATION
Wheelchairs: Accommodated
Disabled Toilets: Yes
The Blind: No Special Facilities

ADMISSION INFO (1996/97 PRICES)
Adult Standing: £4.00
Adult Seating: £5.00
Child Standing: £2.00
Child Seating: £3.00
Concessionary Standing: £2.00
Concessionary Seating: £3.00
Programme Price: £1.00
FAX Number: (01504) 373677

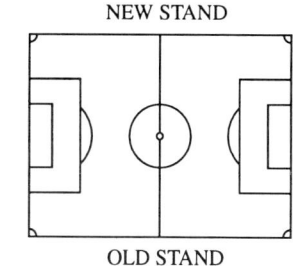

NEW STAND

OLD STAND

Travelling Supporters Information:
Routes: The Stadium is situated over the Craigavon Bridge in the Brandywell area of the city, just to the south of the Bogside. Cross the Craigavon Bridge and take the Abercorn Rd to Bishop Street Without. Pass College on right and continue along to junction with Lone Moor Road. Turn right and ground is on right-hand side of road past Sports Centre.

DUNDALK FC

Founded: 1919
Former Name(s): G. N. R.
Nickname: 'Lillywhites'
Ground: Oriel Park, Dundalk, Co. Louth, Republic of Ireland
Ground No.: (042) 35398/35894
Record Attendance: 22,000
Colours: Shirts - White
        Shorts - Black

Contact No.: (042) 35894
Pitch Size: 98 x 78 yds
Ground Capacity: 20,400
Seating Capacity: 1,600
Correspondence Address: c/o Ms. Elizabeth Duffy, 183 Ard Easmuinn, Dundalk, Co. Louth, Republic of Ireland

GENERAL INFORMATION
Supporters Club Administrator: S. Bellew
Address: c/o. Club
Telephone Number: (042) 35398
Car Parking: Street parking
Coach Parking: At ground
Nearest Railway Station: Dundalk
Nearest Bus Station: Dundalk
Club Shop: Yes
Opening Times: Matchdays only
Telephone No.: (042) 35398
Postal Sales: Yes
Nearest Garda Station: Dundalk
Garda Telephone No.: (042) 35577

DISABLED SUPPORTERS INFORMATION
Wheelchairs: Accommodated
Disabled Toilets: None
The Blind: No Special Facilities

ADMISSION INFO (1996/97 PRICES)
Adult Standing: £4.00
Adult Seating: £6.00
Child Standing: £2.00
Child Seating: £3.00
Concessionary Standing: £2.00
Concessionary Seating: £3.00
Programme Price: £1.00
FAX Number: (042) 30003

CAR PARK STAND

CARRICK END

TOWN END

P. A. BOX
COVERED TERRACING

Travelling Supporters Information:
Routes: Travelling from the north pass through town centre turn right at fourth traffic lights, take second exit at roundabout past 'Harp Brewery' which is on your right and Oriel Park is on the left approx. 200m. Approaching from Carrickmacross Oriel Park is on the right hand side at town boundary. Approaching from Dublin turn left at third traffic lights, 2nd exit at roundabout, (follow same approach as from north). Approaching from Ardee, turn left at Crescent Garda Barracks, past 'Harps Brewery', Oriel Park is on left approx 200m

FINN HARPS FC

Founded: 1954
Former Name(s): None
Nickname: 'Harps'
Ground: Finn Park, Ballybofey, Co. Donegal, Republic of Ireland
Ground No.: (074) 31228
Record Attendance: 8,000 (v Cork Hibernians)
Colours: Shirts - Blue & White
   Shorts - Blue

Contact No.: (074) 31894 (Home); (074) 31053 (Business)
Pitch Size: 130 x 90 yds
Ground Capacity: 8,000
Seating Capacity: 450
Correspondence Address: Pat Gallen, c/o Club

GENERAL INFORMATION
Supporters Club Administrator: None
Address:
Telephone Number:
Car Parking: At Ground
Coach Parking: Adjacent
Nearest Railway Station: Sligo (50 Miles)
Nearest Bus Station: Ballybofey
Club Shop: Yes
Opening Times: Matchdays Only
Telephone No.:
Postal Sales: Yes
Nearest Garda Station: Ballybofey (adjacent)
Garda Telephone No.: (074) 31002

DISABLED SUPPORTERS INFORMATION
Wheelchairs: Accommodated
Disabled Toilets: None
The Blind: No Special Facilities

ADMISSION INFO (1996/97 PRICES)
Adult Standing: £5.00
Adult Seating: £6.00
Child Standing: £2.00 (Under 12's Free)
Child Seating: £3.00
Concessionary Standing: £2.00
Concessionary Seating: £3.00
Programme Price: £1.00
FAX Number: (074) 32387

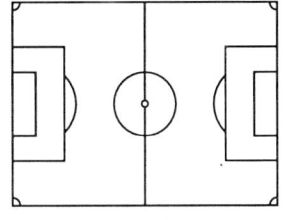

SOCIAL COVERED
CLUB   TERRACING

Travelling Supporters Information:
Routes: Take the N15 from Londonderry into Ballybofey village centre. Turn left at 'Options' shop into Navenny Street and Ground is on left hand side.

HOME FARM EVERTON FC

Founded: 1928
Former Name(s): 'Home Farm Drumcondra FC & Home Farm FC.
Nickname: 'Farm'
Ground: Whitehall, Swords Road, Dublin 9, Republic of Ireland
Ground No.: (01) 371001
Record Attendance: 1,500
Colours: Shirts - Blue & White Hoops
Shorts - Blue
Contact No.: (01) 8756240
Pitch Size: 110 x 75yds
Ground Capacity: 3,500
Seating Capacity: None
Correspondence Address:
c/o Rowan Seery, 97A Swords Road, Dublin 9, Republic of Ireland

GENERAL INFORMATION
Supporters Club Administrator: Rowan Seery
Address: As above
Telephone Number: –
Car Parking: 150 spaces at ground
Coach Parking: At ground
Nearest Railway Station: Dublin Connolly Street Station
Nearest Bus Station: Amiens Street
Club Shop: Yes
Opening Times: Matchdays only
Telephone No.: None
Postal Sales: Yes
Nearest Garda Station: Adjacent
Garda Telephone No.: (01) 8301720

DISABLED SUPPORTERS INFORMATION
Wheelchairs: Accommodated
Disabled Toilets: None
The Blind: No Special Facilities

ADMISSION INFO (1996/97 PRICES)
Adult Standing: £4.00
Child Standing: £1.00
Concessionary Standing: £1.00
Programme Price: £1.00
FAX Number: (01) 8367821

SOCIAL CLUB
COVERED STAND

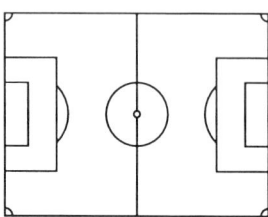

Travelling Supporters Information:
Routes: Ground is situated on main N1 (Swords Road) opposite Highfield Mental Hospital (Just near M1).

ST. PATRICK'S ATHLETIC FC

Founded: 1929
Former Name(s): St. Patrick's FC
Nickname: 'The Saints'
Ground: Richmond Park, Inchicore, Dublin 8, Republic of Ireland
Record Attendance: 13,000
Colours: Shirts - Red
Shorts - White

Contact No.: (01) 4546332
Pitch Size: 110x72yds
Ground Capacity: 7,000
Seating Capacity: 560
Correspondence Address: Club Secretary, 125 Emmet Road, Inchicore, Dublin, Republic of Ireland

GENERAL INFORMATION
Telephone Number:(01) 4546332
Car Parking: At Ground
Coach Parking: At Ground
Nearest Railway Station: 1 Mile
Nearest Bus Station: 1 Mile – 3 buses stop outside ground No. 78, 51, 69
Club Shop: Yes
Opening Times: Matchdays
Telephone No.: As above
Postal Sales: As above
Nearest Garda Station: 500 yds
Garda Telephone No.: (01) 8301720

DISABLED SUPPORTERS INFORMATION
Wheelchairs: Accommodated
Disabled Toilets: Yes
The Blind: No Special Facilities

ADMISSION INFO (1996/97 PRICES)
Adult Standing: £4.00
Adult Seating: £5.00
Child Standing: £2.00
Child Seating: £5.00
Concessionary Standing: £3.00
Concessionary Seating: £4.00
Programme Price: £1.00
FAX Number: (01) 4546211

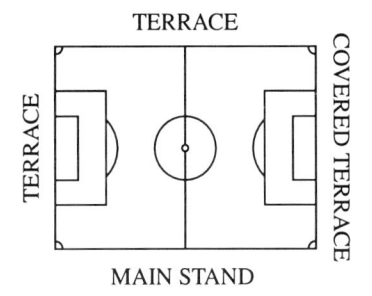

Travelling Supporters Information:
Routes: The Ground is situated to the south of Phoenix Park. Take South Circular Road over Sarah Bridge, then turn 3rd right into Emmet Road. Ground is then on right hand side of road.

SHAMROCK ROVERS FC

Founded: 1901
Former Name(s): None
Nickname: 'The Hoops'
Ground: Royal Dublin Society (RDS), Ballsbridge, Dublin 4, Republic of Ireland
Record Attendance: 22,000
Colours: Shirts - Green & White Hoops
Shorts - Green

Contact No.: (01) 6685433
Pitch Size: 110 x 75 yds
Ground Capacity: 14,000
Seating Capacity: 7,000
Correspondence Address: Paul Doolan, 34 Edmondstown Green, Rathfarnham, Dublin 16, Republic of Ireland

GENERAL INFORMATION
Supporters Club Administrator: Paul Clayton
Address: 2 South Dock Place, Ringstend, Dublin 4
Telephone Number: (01) 6603185
Car Parking: Opposite ground
Coach Parking: Opposite ground
Nearest Railway Station: Lansdowne Road
Nearest Bus Station: Dublin
Club Shop: Yes
Opening Times: Matchdays only
Telephone No.: (087) 551620
Postal Sales: Yes
Nearest Garda Station: Donnybrook
Garda Telephone No.: (01) 2693766

DISABLED SUPPORTERS INFORMATION
Wheelchairs: Accommodated
Disabled Toilets: None
The Blind: No Special Facilities

ADMISSION INFO (1996/97 PRICES)
Adult Standing: £4.00
Adult Seating: £4.00
Child Standing: £2.00
Child Seating: £2.00
Concessionary Standing: £2.00
Concessionary Seating: £2.00
Programme Price: £1.00
FAX Number: (01) 4545114

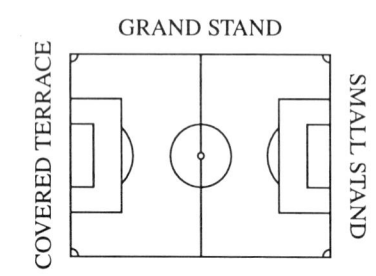

Travelling Supporters Information:
Routes: Take the N11 to Ballsbridge and turn by bus depot into Anglesea Road. Ground is adjacent to the junction with Simmonscourt Road at the rear of the Royal Dublin Society's Premises.

SHELBOURNE FC

Founded: 1895
Former Name(s): None
Nickname: 'Shels', 'The Reds'
Ground: Tolka Park, Richmond Road, Drumcondra, Dublin 3, Republic of Ireland
Ground No.: (01) 837575
Record Attendance: 9,000 (v Bohemian 1993)
Colours: Shirts - Red
　　　　　　Shorts - Red

Contact No.: (01) 8375536/8375754
Pitch Size: 110 x 75 yds
Ground Capacity: 9,200 (all seats)
Correspondence Address: Oliver Byrne, Secretary, c/o Tolka Park, Richmond Road, Dublin, Republic of Ireland

GENERAL INFORMATION
Supporters Club Administrator: Niall Fitzmaurice
Address: c/o Club
Telephone Number: (01) 8388761
Car Parking: Street Parking
Coach Parking: Street Parking
Nearest Railway Station: Amiens Street
Nearest Bus Station: Buses to Drumcondra
Club Shop: Yes
Opening Times: Matchdays
Telephone No.: (01) 8375754
Postal Sales: Yes
Nearest Grada Station: Whitehall
Grada Telephone No.: (01) 8374356

DISABLED SUPPORTERS INFORMATION
Wheelchairs: Accommodated
Disabled Toilets: None
The Blind: No Facilities

ADMISSION INFO (1996/97 PRICES)
Adult Seating: £5.00
Child Standing: £2.00
Concessionary Standing: £2.00
Programme Price: £1.00
FAX Number: (01) 8375588

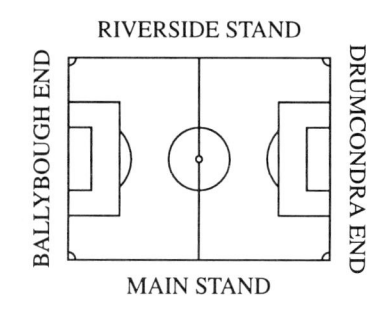

Travelling Supporters Information:
Routes: Take the N1 (Belfast) road from city centre. Ground is situated in Richmond Road adjacent to Holy Cross College over the Drumcondra Bridge

SLIGO ROVERS FC

Founded: 1928
Former Name(s): None
Nickname: 'Rovers', 'The Bit of Red'
Ground: The Showgrounds, Sligo, Co. Sligo, Republic of Ireland
Record Attendance: 9,000 (v Shamrock Rovers 1976/77)
Colours: Shirts - Red & White
Shorts - Red

Contact No.: (071) 71212
Pitch Size: 110 x 75 yds
Ground Capacity: 7,000
Seating Capacity: 700
Correspondence Address:
Stephen McLoughlin, c/o Sligo Rovers FC, P.O. Box 275, Sligo, Republic of Ireland

GENERAL INFORMATION
Supporters Club Administrator: Tommoy Horan
Address: c/o Club
Telephone Number: (071) 71212
Car Parking: None nearby
Coach Parking: Cathedral Street
Nearest Railway Station: Sligo
Nearest Bus Station: Sligo
Club Shop: Yes
Opening Times: Matchdays only
Telephone No.: (071) 71212
Postal Sales: Yes
Nearest Garda Station: Sligo
Garda Telephone No.: (071) 42031

DISABLED SUPPORTERS INFORMATION
Wheelchairs: Accommodated
Disabled Toilets: None
The Blind: No Special Facilities

ADMISSION INFO (1996/97 PRICES)
Adult Standing: £4.50
Adult Seating: £5.50
Child Standing: £3.00
Child Seating: £5.50
Concessionary Standing: £3.00
Concessionary Seating: £5.50
Programme Price: £1.00
FAX Number: (071) 71331

JINKS ROAD STADIUM

STATION END TERRACE

CHURCH HILL END

TRACEY ROAD STAND

Travelling Supporters Information:
Routes: Coming from Derry/Donegal: You come into town on the Ballyshannon Road, cross over river and proceed to traffic lights at Adelaide Street/Wine Street junction. Proceed into Adelaide Street and park at Adelaide Street car park (Dunnes Stores on your left); Coming from Leitrim/Fermanagh: Follow one way traffic system until you reach Wine Street car park, about half way down street; Coming from West, East or South: All roads converge at Ballisodare (5 miles from Sligo), from there drive into town. Proceed down Pearse Road until you reach sign saying 'Heavy Goods Vehicles' this way (Arrow pointing). You go down Mail Coach Road, until you reach traffic lights. Keep going on straight until you reach the Cathedral (on your right), you can park there or go straight on to Adelaide Street and park there; Coming from Adelaide Street/ Wine Street Car Parks: You walk up towards Cathedral, when you reach traffic lights you turn right into John Street and walk straight on up to ground; Coming from Cathedral: Turn left into John Street at traffic lights; Coming from Railway/Bus Station: Cross road into Wolfe Tone Street and walk to end and turn right and on up to the ground.

UNIVERSITY COLLEGE DUBLIN FC

Founded: 1895-1908
Former Name(s): Catholic University FC
Nickname: 'The Students'
Ground: Belfield Park, Stillorgan, Dublin 4, Republic of Ireland
Record Attendance: 3,750
Colours: Shirts - Sky Blue
Shorts - Sky Blue

Contact No.: (01) 2601155 (Club Secretary) or (01) 7062183
Pitch Size: 115 x 70 yds
Ground Capacity: 4,000
Seating Capacity: 500
Correspondence Address: Program Editor – Declan Hughes, 9 Tara Lawn, The Donahies, Dublin 13, Republic of Ireland

GENERAL INFORMATION
Supporters Club Administrator: Padraig Keane
Address: Pinewood Park, Dublin 14
Telephone Number: (01) 4932768
Car Parking: On Campus
Coach Parking: On Campus
Nearest Railway Station: Dublin
Nearest Bus Station: Dublin
Club Shop: Yes
Opening Times: Matchdays Only
Telephone No.: (01) 2894444
Postal Sales: Yes
Nearest Garda Station: Donnybrook
Garda Telephone No.: (01) 2693766

DISABLED SUPPORTERS INFORMATION
Wheelchairs: Accommodated
Disabled Toilets: None
The Blind: No Special Facilities

ADMISSION INFO (1996/97 PRICES)
Adult Standing: £4.00
Adult Seating: £4.00
Child Standing: £2.00
Child Seating: £2.00
Concessionary Standing: £2.00
Concessionary Seating: £2.00
Programme Price: £1.00
FAX Number: (01) 2698099

COVERED STAND

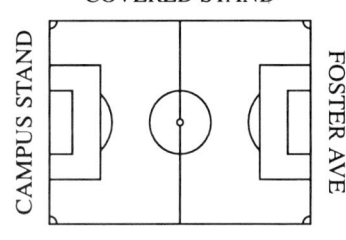

CAMPUS STAND

FOSTER AVE

P.A. BOX/T.V.TOWER
OPEN BANK

Travelling Supporters Information:
Routes: Take the N11 (Bray Road) south from city centre. By University campus turn into Foster's Avenue and entrance to the park is first entrance on right after passing North Avenue on left.

ATHLONE TOWN FC

Founded: 1887
Former Name(s): None
Nickname: 'Town'
Ground: St. Mel's Park, Athlone, Co. Westmeath, Republic of Ireland
Record Attendance: Not known
Colours: Shirts - Blue & Black Stripes
Shorts - Black

Contact No.: (0902) 75268
Pitch Size: 110 x 71 yds
Ground Capacity: 10,000
Seating Capacity: 200
Correspondence Address:
c/o Jack McKervey, 7 St. Frances Terrace, Athlone, Republic of Ireland

GENERAL INFORMATION
Supporters Club Administrator: None
Address: –
Telephone Number: –
Car Parking: Small car park at ground
Coach Parking: In Town
Nearest Railway Station: Athlone (0.25 mile)
Nearest Bus Station: Athlone (0.25 mile)
Club Shop: No
Opening Times: –
Telephone No.: –
Postal Sales: –
Nearest Garda Station: Athlone (1 mile)
Grada Telephone No.: (0902) 92609

DISABLED SUPPORTERS INFORMATION
Wheelchairs: Accommodated at pitch side
Disabled Toilets: None
The Blind: No Special Facilities

ADMISSION INFO (1996/97 PRICES)
Adult Standing: £4.00
Child Standing: £2.00
Concessionary Standing: £2.00
Programme Price: £1.00
FAX Number: (0902) 21119

COVERED SIDE

COVERED TERRACE

Travelling Supporters Information:
Routes: Take the N55/N6/N61 to Athlone. The ground is situated just off the N55 to the north of the town. Exit from the N55 at junction 4 and turn left, then turn off at mini-roundabout into Grace Park Road and pass under railway bridge. Bear left at end and ground is on right.

COBH RAMBLERS FC

Founded: 1922
Former Name(s): Cove Ramblers
Nickname: 'Ramblers' or 'The Rams'
Ground: St. Colmans Park, Cobh, Co. Cork, Republic Of Ireland
Ground No.: (021) 812371
Record Attendance: 6,612 (v Finn Harps 1983)
Colours: Shirts - Claret & Blue
　　　　　 Shorts - White

Pitch Size: 108 x 78 yds
Ground Capacity: 10,000
Seating Capacity: Under Construction
Correspondence Address: Michael Geasley, 1A Casement Square, Cobh, Co. Cork, Republic of Ireland
Phone No.: (021) 813189
Contact No.: (021) 811412

GENERAL INFORMATION
Supporters Club Administrator: Michael Geasley
Address: –
Telephone Number: (021) 813189
Car Parking: Street parking
Coach Parking: At ground
Nearest Railway Station: Cobh
Nearest Bus Station: Cork
Club Shop: None
Opening Times: –
Telephone No.: –
Postal Sales: –
Nearest Garda Station: Cobh
Garda Telephone No.: (021) 811333

DISABLED SUPPORTERS INFORMATION
Wheelchairs: Accommodated
Disabled Toilets: None
The Blind: No Special Facilities

ADMISSION INFO (1996/97 PRICES)
Adult Standing: £3.00
Child Standing: £1.00
Concessionary Standing: £1.50
Programme Price: £1.00
FAX Number: (021) 811412

COVERED SIDE

(SOCIAL CLUB) COVERED END

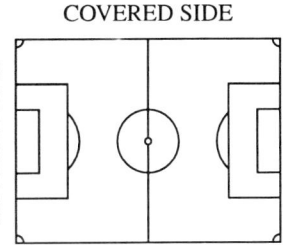

Travelling Supporters Information:
Routes: Approaching from Cork City or Waterford: Branch off before Carrigtwohill village on dual carriageway roundabout to Cobh and keep right to Belvelly bridge just beyond Fota Wildlife Park entry. Turn right, and keep right for 4.5 miles, in the process passing IFI Fertilizer Plant and Verolme Dockyard. Take second left beyond Statiol Filling Station on the Lake Road and follow direct route for 0.5 mile on rising ground. On reaching level and fourth such exit on left side, St. Colman's Park is visible by floodlight pylons.

DROGHEDA UNITED FC

Founded: 1919
Former Name(s): None
Nickname: 'United'
Ground: United Park, Drogheda, Co. Louth, Republic of Ireland
Ground No.: (041) 30190
Record Attendance: 6,000
Colours: Shirts - Maroon & Blue
Shorts - White

Contact No.: (041) 30190
Pitch Size: 110x75 yds
Ground Capacity: 6,000
Seating Capacity: 396
Correspondence Address: Anna McKenna, Admin. Secretary, c/o Club

GENERAL INFORMATION
Supporters Club Administrator: C. Hurley
Address: 38 Hillview, Rathmullen, Drogheda, Co. Louth, Republic of Ireland
Telephone Number: (041) 31267
Car Parking: At Ground
Coach Parking: At Ground
Nearest Railway Station: Drogheda
Nearest Bus Station: Drogheda
Club Shop: Yes
Opening Times: Prior to and during matches
Telephone No.: –
Postal Sales: –
Nearest Garda Station: Drogheda
Garda Telephone No.: (041) 38777

DISABLED SUPPORTERS INFORMATION
Wheelchairs: Accommodated
Disabled Toilets: Yes
The Blind: No Special Facilities

ADMISSION INFO (1996/97 PRICES)
Adult Standing: £4.00
Adult Seating: £5.00
Child Standing: £3.00
Child Seating: £5.00
Programme Price: £1.00
FAX Number: (041) 30190

TV GANTRY
COVERED TERRACE

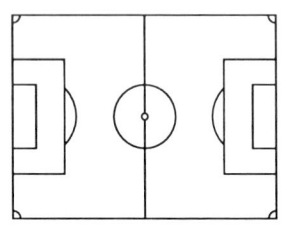

CLUB HSE   COVERED TERRACE
SEATED STAND

Travelling Supporters Information:
Routes: The ground is situated in the north of Drogheda near 'Our Lady of Lourdes International Training Hospital'.

GALWAY UNITED FC

Founded: 1937
Former Name(s): 'Galway Rovers'
Nickname: The Tribesmen
Ground: Terryland Park, Dyke Road, Galway, Republic of Ireland
Record Attendance: 7,260 (v. Cork City 1994)
Colours: Shirts - Maroon & Sky Blue
　　　　　Shorts - White

Contact No.: (091) 561000
Pitch Size: 110 x 75 yds
Ground Capacity: 8,000
Seating Capacity: 1,400 (when new stand complete)
Correspondence Address: c/o Paul O' Brien, 22 William Street, Galway, Republic of Ireland

GENERAL INFORMATION
Supporters Club Administrator: Pat Kelly
Address: c/o Club
Telephone Number: (091) 841795
Car Parking: 200 spaces at ground
Coach Parking: At ground
Nearest Railway Station: Ceannt Station (1.5 miles)
Nearest Bus Station: Eyre Square (1.5 miles)
Club Shop: Yes
Opening Times: Matchdays Only
Telephone No.: (091) 561000
Postal Sales: Yes
Nearest Garda Station: Mill Street (2 miles)
Garda Telephone No.: (091) 563161

DISABLED SUPPORTERS INFORMATION
Wheelchairs: Accommodated
Disabled Toilets: Yes
The Blind: No Special Facilities

ADMISSION INFO (1996/97 PRICES)
Adult Standing: £4.00
Adult Seating: £5.00
Child Standing: £3.00
Child Seating: £4.00
Concessionary Standing: £2.00
Concessionary Seating: N/A
Programme Price: £1.00
FAX Number: (091) 561000

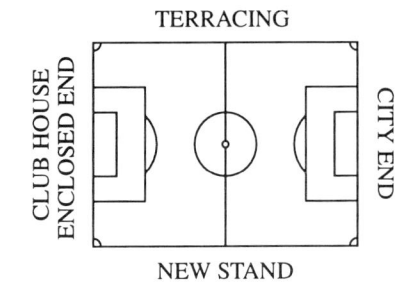

Travelling Supporters Information:
Routes: Follow N6 dual carriageway to roundabout at Terryland Shopping Centre (Dunnes Stores). Take second exit onto Headford Road, first right after McDonalds Drive Thru' and Omniplex Cinema. Pass the Blackbox Theatre. Ground is at top of this road after travelling under flyover, Terryland Park is on the right.

KILKENNY CITY FC

Founded: 1966
Former Name(s): 'Emfa FC'
Nickname: 'The Cats'
Ground: Buckley Park, Tennypark, Callan Road, Kilkenny, Co. Kilkenny, Republic of Ireland
Ground No.: (056) 51888
Record Attendance: 6,500

Colours: Shirts - Amber
Shorts - Black
Contact No.: (056) 22717
Pitch Size: 107 x 78 yds
Ground Capacity: 7,000
Seating Capacity: 1,000
Correspondence Address: c/o Jim Rhatigan, 7 Cedarwood Close, Loughboy, Kilkenny, Republic of Ireland

GENERAL INFORMATION
Supporters Club Administrator: None
Address: –
Telephone Number: –
Car Parking: Street parking
Coach Parking: At ground (inside ground minibuses only)
Nearest Railway Station: Kilkenny (2.5 mls)
Nearest Bus Station: Kilkenny (2.5 miles)
Club Shop: Yes
Opening Times: Matchdays Only
Telephone No.: (056) 51888
Postal Sales: Yes
Nearest Garda Station: Kilkenny City (2 miles)
Garda Telephone No.: (056) 22222

DISABLED SUPPORTERS INFORMATION
Wheelchairs: Accommodated in front of stand
Disabled Toilets: None
The Blind: No Special Facilities

ADMISSION INFO (1996/97 PRICES)
Adult Standing: £4.00
Adult Seating: £5.00
Child Standing: £2.00
Child Seating: £3.00
Concessionary Standing: £2.00
Concessionary Seating: £3.00
Programme Price: £1.00
FAX Number: (056) 21414

SMALL SEATED AREA

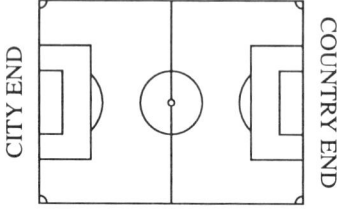

CITY END

COUNTRY END

MAIN STAND

Travelling Supporters Information:
Routes: Buckley Park is on the N76 Callan/Clonmel Road 1.5 miles outside of the city.

LIMERICK FC

Founded: 1983
Former Name(s): 'Limerick City'
Nickname: Blues
Ground: Rathbane North, Limerick, Republic of Ireland
Ground No.: (061) 47874
Record Attendance: 5,500
Colours: Shirts - Blue
Shorts - White

Contact No.: (061) 340264
Pitch Size: 115 x 76 yds
Ground Capacity: 10,000
Seating Capacity: None
Correspondence Address: c/o Noel Hanley, 16 Athlunkard Close, Shannon Banks, Corbally, Limerick City, Republic of Ireland
Tel: (061) 340264 (Home); (061) 417844 (Business)

GENERAL INFORMATION

Supporters Club Administrator: Jimmy Mulready
Address: 15 Riverglen, Crossagalla, Old Cork Road, Limerick
Telephone Number: (061) 415478
Car Parking: At Ground
Coach Parking: At Ground
Nearest Railway Station: Colbert (1.5 miles)
Nearest Bus Station: Colbert
Club Shop: Yes
Opening Times: Matchdays Only
Telephone No.: None
Postal Sales: No
Nearest Garda Station: Roxboro
Garda Telephone No.: (061) 419555

DISABLED SUPPORTERS INFORMATION

Wheelchairs: Accommodated
Disabled Toilets: None
The Blind: No Special Facilities

ADMISSION INFO (1996/97 PRICES)

Adult Standing: £4.00
Child Standing: £2.00
Concessionary Standing: £2.00
Programme Price: None, but free teamsheets
FAX Number: (061) 330617

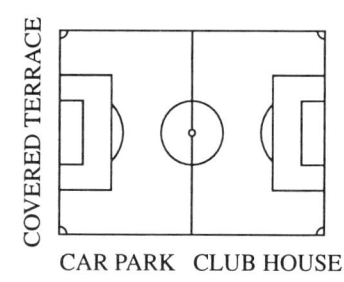

CAR PARK   CLUB HOUSE

Travelling Supporters Information:
Routes: Take the N7 from Dublin into Limerick then turn left at roundabout by Parkway Shopping Centre. Continue straight ahead at next three roundabouts then take the 2nd left at Murphy's Shop and the ground is straight ahead.

LONGFORD TOWN FC

Founded: 1924
Former Name(s): None
Nickname: 'The Town'
Ground: Connaught Road, Longford, Co. Longford, Republic of Ireland
Record Attendance: Not known
Colours: Shirts - Red
　　　　　　Shorts - Black
Ground No.: (043) 46296

Pitch Size: 118 x 90 yds
Ground Capacity: 10,000
Seating Capacity: None
Correspondence Address: Andy Dowd, c/o Longford Arms Hotel, Longford, Republic Of Ireland
Tel: (088) 634439

GENERAL INFORMATION
Supporters Club Administrator: None
Address: –
Telephone Number: –
Car Parking: At Ground
Coach Parking: At Ground
Nearest Railway Station: Longford (2.5 miles)
Nearest Bus Station: Longford (2.5 miles)
Club Shop: None
Opening Times: –
Telephone No.: –
Postal Sales: –
Nearest Garda Station: Dublin Street, Longford (2.5 miles)
Garda Telephone No.: (043) 46741

DISABLED SUPPORTERS INFORMATION
Wheelchairs: Accommodated
Disabled Toilets: None
The Blind: No Special Facilities

ADMISSION INFO (1996/97 PRICES)
Adult Standing: £4.00
Child Standing: £2.00
Concessionary Standing: £2.00
Programme Price: £1.00
FAX Number: None

COVERED TERRACE

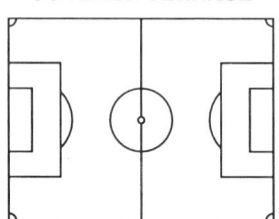

Travelling Supporters Information:
Routes: Take the N4 to Longford. In town centre take the N5 Westbound and the ground is 2.5 miles off main road on left, outside of town.

MONAGHAN UNITED FC

Founded: 1979
Former Name(s):
Nickname: The Trojans
Ground: Gortakeegan, Newbliss Road, Monaghan, Co. Monaghan, Republic of Ireland
Ground No.: (047) 84450
Record Attendance: 2,000
Colours: Shirts - Royal Blue
Shorts - White

Contact No.: (047) 84798
Pitch Size: 110x74 yds
Ground Capacity: 5,000
Seating Capacity: 620
Correspondence Address: c/o Club

GENERAL INFORMATION
Supporters Club Administrator: Martin Monahan
Address: Old Cross Square, Monaghan, Republic of Ireland
Telephone Number: (047) 84435
Car Parking: Yes
Coach Parking: Yes
Nearest Railway Station: Dundalk 32 miles
Nearest Bus Station: 1 Mile
Club Shop: Yes
Opening Times: Matchdays Only
Telephone No.: –
Postal Sales: No
Nearest Garda Station: Monaghan (1 mile)
Garda Telephone No.: (047)82222

DISABLED SUPPORTERS INFORMATION
Wheelchairs: Accommodated
Disabled Toilets: Yes
The Blind: No Special Facilities

ADMISSION INFO (1996/97 PRICES)
Adult Standing: £4.00
Adult Seating: £5.00
Child Standing: £2.00
Child Seating: £3.00
Programme Price: £1.00
FAX Number: (047) 84798

CAR PARK
CLUB HOUSE   STAND
ROSSMORE END
TOWN END
KILLYCONIGAN END
& TRAINNIG PITCHES

Travelling Supporters Information:
Routes: The Ground is 1 mile from Monaghan town on N54 to Clones. Turn left for Threemilehouse/Newbliss, then ground is 100 yards along on left.

ST. JAMES'S GATE FC

Founded: 1902
Former Name(s): None
Nickname: 'The Gate'
Ground: Iveagh Grounds, Crumlin, Dublin 12, Republic of Ireland
Record Attendance: 28,000
Colours: Shirts - Red
　　　　　　Shorts - Green

Contact No.: (01) 4597883 (Club Secretary)
Pitch Size: 120 x 75 yds
Ground Capacity: 3,000
Seating Capacity: None
Correspondence Address: c/o Gerry Juhel, 26 Woodbank Avenue, Dublin 11, Republic of Ireland

GENERAL INFORMATION
Supporters Club Administrator: Mark Howell
Address: Premier Information, South Dock Road, Ringsend, Dublin 4
Telephone Number: (01) 6670011
Car Parking: At ground
Coach Parking: At ground
Nearest Railway Station: City Centre
Nearest Bus Station: City Centre Nos. 150, 50, 50A, 77, 77A all pass the ground
Club Shop: None
Opening Times: –
Telephone No.: –
Postal Sales: Yes to Correspondence Address
Nearest Garda Station: Sundrive Road, Dublin 12
Garda Telephone No.: (01) 4555541

DISABLED SUPPORTERS INFORMATION
Wheelchairs: Accommodated
Disabled Toilets: None
The Blind: No Special Facilities

ADMISSION INFO (1996/97 PRICES)
Adult Standing: £4.00
Child Standing: £2.00
Concessionary Standing: £2.00
Programme Price: £1.00
FAX Number: (01) 6670055

OLD STAND (DISUSED)

ELVEDEN PAVILION

BRICKFIELD END

JAM FACTORY SIDE

Travelling Supporters Information:
Routes: From the South: On Naas Rd take turning for Crumlin, straight down Long Mile Rd, continue straight on to Crumlin Road, the Iveagh Ground is on the left side of the road approximately 800m. Beyond the Childrens Hospital; From the North: Use the new link road to bypass the city centre, and on to the M50 take the Crumlin, turn-off and follow the above directions; From the City Centre: Use the South Quays alongside the River Liffey to and around Heuston station to top of road turn left straight up to 4th set of traffic lights on Canal Bridge turn left down to next bridge turn right onto Herberton Road to next set of traffic lights at Crumlin Rd. Turn right, ground is approximately 400m up the road, on right hand side; Public Transport: Use 150 (IMP) from Temple Bare/Fleet Street. Stops across Road from ground or 50, 50A, 77, 77A from Eden Quay (N side River Liffey Bank) as above.

WATERFORD UNITED FC

Founded: 1982
Former Name(s): Waterford FC.
Nickname: 'The Blues'
Ground: Waterford Regional Sports Centre, Cork Road, Waterford, Republic of Ireland
Record Attendance: 6,000
Colours: Shirts - Blue
　　　　　Shorts - Blue/White

Contact No.: (051) 74087
Pitch Size: 100 x 72 yds
Ground Capacity: 8,000
Seating Capacity: 1,200
Correspondence Address:
c/o Michael Butler, 22 Decies Avenue, Lismore Lawn, Waterford, Republic of Ireland

GENERAL INFORMATION
Supporters Club Administrator: Billy McGrath
Address: 25 Glencarra, Waterford
Telephone Number: (051) 53600
Car Parking: Yes 1,000 spaces
Coach Parking: Yes
Nearest Railway Station: Waterford
Nearest Bus Station: Waterford
Club Shop: Yes
Opening Times: Matchdays only
Telephone No.: None
Postal Sales: c/o Supporter Club
Nearest Garda Station: Waterford
Garda Telephone No.: (051) 74888

DISABLED SUPPORTERS INFORMATION
Wheelchairs: Accommodated
Disabled Toilets: Yes
The Blind: No Special Facilities

ADMISSION INFO (1996/97 PRICES)
Adult Standing: £4.00
Adult Seating: £4.00
Child Standing: £2.00
Child Seating: £2.00
Concessionary Standing: £2.00
Concessionary Seating: £2.00
Programme Price: £1.00
FAX Number: (051) 55249

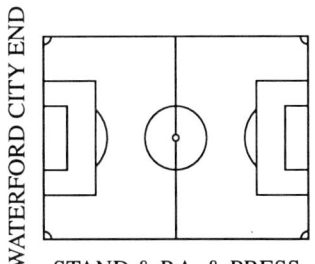

WATERFORD CITY END　　　TRAMORE END

STAND & P.A. & PRESS
COACH & CAR PARK

Travelling Supporters Information:
Routes: Take the N9 to Waterford then from train station and bus depot cross over Rice Bridge. Turn left along the Quay and Parnell Street and out onto the main Waterford-Cork Road. The ground is situated on the left half a mile out.

STATISTICS SEASON 1995-96

Contents:

Bord Gáis FAI Premier Division
Home & Away Chart
Final Table

Bord Gáis FAI First Division
Home & Away Chart
Final Table

Bord Gáis FAI National League Premier Division 1995/96 Season	Athlone Town	Bohemians	Cork City	Derry City	Drogheda United	Dundalk	Galway United	St. Patrick's Athletic	Shamrock Rovers	Shelbourne	Sligo Rovers	UCD
Athlone Town		2-5	2-4	1-1	0-2	0-0	0-2	0-1	2-0	1-2	1-2	1-0
		0-3			0-0	1-0	2-2		4-3			
Bohemians	3-1		1-1	1-0	6-0	3-2	3-0	0-1	1-1	1-0	2-0	0-0
			1-0	1-1				0-0	1-0		1-2	3-1
Cork City	2-0	1-0		0-1	1-2	0-2	1-1	1-0	2-0	1-1	2-1	2-1
	0-2				2-1		3-0	0-0		2-1		
Derry City	5-3	1-1	2-0		1-0	1-1	2-0	5-1	1-1	1-2	1-2	3-1
	1-1		2-1		1-1	0-1				4-0	0-0	
Drogheda United	0-1	2-5	2-2	2-2		3-2	3-0	1-3	1-2	1-1	0-0	0-1
	0-1	0-1				2-1	6-0		1-3	0-1		
Dundalk	2-1	1-2	0-0	2-*1	2-2		2-0	3-2	1-0	1-1	0-1	2-0
		2-4	0-1				1-2	0-0		0-1		
Galway United	2-2	1-5	3-1	1-1	0-3	0-1		0-1	1-1	1-1	2-3	1-1
		0-2		0-3		2-1			0-2	1-3		0-2
St. Patrick's Athletic	3-2	3-3	2-1	3-3	1-0	2-1	1-2		1-0	2-1	1-0	2-1
		0-2		0-3		2-1			0-2	1-3		0-2
Shamrock Rovers	1-1	1-0	1-1	2-0	1-1	1-0	2-1	0-1		0-1	0-2	0-2
	2-1		2-0	2-1	1-0						2-0	
Shelbourne	1-0	1-0	1-1	1-2	0-0	3-1	2-0	1-1	3-0		0-0	1-1
		1-0		1-0		0-1		1-2			2-1	
Sligo Rovers	4-2	0-0	3-1	1-1	1-0	3-3	3-2	0-0	0-1	0-1		2-0
	2-1		4-1				0-2	1-1	3-1			
UCD	3-0	3-1	0-1	2-0	0-0	1-2	2-0	0-2	0-1	0-3	2-1	
	1-2		2-1			4-1	0-0			3-2	3-1	

BORD GÁIS FAI PREMIER DIVISION 1995/96
LEAGUE TABLE FINAL

St. Patrick's Athletic	33	19	10	4	53	34	67
Bohemians	33	18	8	7	60	29	62
Sligo Rovers	33	16	7	10	45	38	55
Shelbourne	33	15	9	9	45	33	54
Shamrock Rovers	33	14	8	11	32	32	50
Derry City	33	11	13	9	50	38	46
Dundalk	33	11	9	13	38	39	42
UCD	33	12	6	15	38	40	42
Cork City	33	12	8	13	37	41	41 *
Athlone Town	33	8	7	18	38	59	31
Drogheda United	33	7	9	17	39	51	30
Galway United	33	5	6	22	26	67	21

* Cork City were had 3 points deducted for fielding unregistered players

Relegated: - Galway United, Drogheda United and Athlone Town

Bord Gáis FAI National League First Division 1995/96 Season	Bray Wanderers	Cobh Ramblers	Finn Harps	Home Farm Everton	Kilkenny City	Limerick	Longford Town	Monaghan United	St. James's Gate	Waterford United
Bray Wanderers		0-0	4-0	4-1	3-1	1-1	3-1	5-0	5-1	3-0
		0-0	0-2			1-1			0-0	
Cobh Ramblers	0-0		1-1	4-0	1-1	1-0	1-0	2-2	1-0	1-1
			4-0	0-0			0-1		0-0	0-0
Finn Harps	0-1	1-1		1-1	1-1	1-0	3-0	2-0	3-3	1-1
							2-0		7-0	3-0	3-0
Home Farm Everton	0-1	3-1	1-0		3-1	1-2	2-1	3-0	1-3	4-1
	4-0		0-0			1-0		1-0		3-1
Kilkenny City	0-2	0-3	0-2			0-1	3-0	2-1	1-1	1-0
	2-2	2-0	2-1	2-2		2-0		1-1		
Limerick	1-2	0-2	1-4	2-1	1-2		0-2	5-0	1-1	3-1
		1-0		3-0					0-0	2-0
Longford Town	0-3	0-1	2-5	1-3	2-4	1-1		0-0	1-1	1-2
	1-3		0-1		1-1	1-4			1-1	
Monaghan United	1-5	0-3	0-4	2-5	0-1	1-0	0-4		1-3	0-2
	0-3	0-1		0-1			1-0			0-0
St. James's Gate	2-0	0-0	1-0	1-2	2-2	0-0	0-1	4-0		2-1
				2-0	3-1		2-0			1-1
Waterford United	1-2	2-2	1-2	1-0	2-0	5-1	1-3	5-0	2-1	
	1-0				2-0	2-5	1-1			

BORD GÁIS FAI 1ST DIVISION 1995/96

LEAGUE TABLE FINAL

Bray Wanderers	27	16	7	4	53	21	55
Finn Harps	27	14	7	6	50	25	49
Home Farm-Everton	27	14	4	9	42	34	46
Cobh Ramblers	27	10	13	4	30	15	43
St. James's Gate	27	9	11	7	35	30	38
Limerick	27	10	6	11	37	34	36
Kilkenny City	27	9	8	10	33	38	35
Waterford United	27	9	7	11	37	40	34
Longford Town	27	5	6	16	26	46	21
Monaghan United	27	2	5	20	10	70	11

Promoted: - Bray Wanderers, Finn Harps and Home Farm-Everton

Promotion/Relegation play-off
Home Farm-Everton 2   Athlone Town.........................0
Athlone Town 2   Home Farm-Everton.............0

Aggregate 2-2. Home Farm-Everton won 4-3 on penalties and were promoted

EIRE INTERNATIONAL LINE-UPS AND STATISTICS 1995

29th March 1995
v NORTHERN IRELAND *Dublin*
A. Kelly 2	Sheffield United
G. Kelly	Leeds United
D. Irwin	Manchester United
P. McGrath	Aston Villa
P. Babb	Liverpool
J. Sheridan	Sheffield Wednesday
A. Townsend	Aston Villa
R. Keane	Manchester United
S. Staunton	Aston Villa
N. Quinn †	Manchester City
D. Kelly *	Wolverhampton Wanderers

Result 1-1 N. Quinn
Sub: J. McAteer *, A. Cascarino †

26th April 1995
v PORTUGAL *Dublin*
A. Kelly 2	Sheffield United
G. Kelly	Leeds United
D. Irwin	Manchester United
P. Babb	Liverpool
P. McGrath	Aston Villa
R. Houghton †	Crystal Palace
A. Townsend	Aston Villa
J. Sheridan	Sheffield Wednesday
S. Staunton	Aston Villa
N. Quinn	Manchester City
J. Aldridge *	Tranmere Rovers

Result 1-0 S. Staunton
Sub: A. Cascarino *, J. Kenna †

3rd June 1995
v LIECHTENSTEIN *Vaduz*
A. Kelly 2	Sheffield United
G. Kelly	Leeds United
D. Irwin	Manchester United
P. Babb	Liverpool
P. McGrath	Aston Villa
R. Whelan 2	Southend United
J. McAteer †	Bolton Wanderers
J. Sheridan	Sheffield Wednesday
S. Staunton	Aston Villa
N. Quinn *	Manchester City
J. Aldridge	Tranmere Rovers

Result 0-0
Sub: A. Cascarino *, J. Kenna †

11th June 1995
v AUSTRIA *Dublin*
A. Kelly 2	Sheffield United
G. Kelly	Leeds United
D. Irwin	Manchester United
P. Babb	Liverpool
P. McGrath	Aston Villa
R. Whelan 2	Southend United
R. Houghton	Crystal Palace
J. Sheridan	Sheffield Wednesday
S. Staunton *	Aston Villa
T. Coyne	Motherwell
N. Quinn †	Manchester City

Result 1-3 R. Houghton
Sub: J. Kenna *, A. Cascarino †

6th September 1995
v AUSTRIA *Vienna*
A. Kelly 2	Sheffield United
G. Kelly	Leeds United
D. Irwin	Manchester United
A. Kernaghan	Manchester City
P. McGrath	Aston Villa
R. Houghton *	Crystal Palace
A. Townsend	Aston Villa
R. Keane	Manchester United
J. Sheridan	Sheffield Wednesday
M. Kennedy 2	Liverpool
N. Quinn	Manchester City

Result 1-3 P. McGrath
Sub: A. Cascarino *

11th October 1995
v LATVIA *Dublin*
A. Kelly 2	Sheffield United
G. Kelly	Leeds United
T. Phelan	Manchester City
P. Babb	Liverpool
P. McGrath	Aston Villa
J. McAteer	Liverpool
A. Townsend	Aston Villa
J. Kenna	Blackburn Rovers
S. Staunton	Aston Villa
N. Quinn	Manchester City
J. Aldridge	Tranmere Rovers

Result 2-1 J. Aldridge 2 (1 pen)

15th November 1995
v PORTUGAL *Lisbon*
A. Kelly 2	Sheffield United
G. Kelly	Leeds United
D. Irwin	Manchester United
P. Babb	Liverpool
P. McGrath	Aston Villa
J. McAteer	Liverpool
M. Kennedy 2 *	Liverpool
J. Kenna	Blackburn Rovers
S. Staunton †	Aston Villa
N. Quinn	Manchester City
J. Aldridge	Tranmere Rovers

Result 0-3
Sub: A. Cascarino *, A. Kernaghan †

13th December 1995
v HOLLAND *Liverpool*
A. Kelly 2	Sheffield United
G. Kelly	Leeds United
D. Irwin	Manchester United
P. Babb	Liverpool
P. McGrath	Aston Villa
J. Kenna	Blackburn Rovers
A. Townsend *	Aston Villa
J. Sheridan	Sheffield Wednesday
T. Phelan	Chelsea
J. Aldridge †	Tranmere Rovers
A. Cascarino	Marseille

Result 0-2
Sub: J. McAteer *, A. Kernaghan †

EIRE INTERNATIONAL LINE-UPS AND STATISTICS 1996

27th March 1996
v RUSSIA *Dublin*
S. Given	Blackburn Rovers
T. Phelan	Chelsea
S. Staunton	Aston Villa
A. Kernaghan	Manchester City
P. McGrath	Aston Villa
R. Keane	Manchester United
A. Townsend *	Aston Villa
J. McAteer	Liverpool
N. Quinn °	Manchester City
J. Aldridge †	Tranmere Rovers
M. Kennedy 2	Liverpool

Result 0-2
*Sub: J. Kenna *, A. Cascarino †, T. Coyne °*

24th April 1996
v CZECH REPUBLIC *Prague*
S. Given	Blackburn Rovers
J. Kenna	Blackburn Rovers
D. Irwin *	Manchester United
K. Cunningham	Wimbledon
P. Babb †	Liverpool
P. McGrath	Aston Villa
R. Houghton	Crystal Palace
M. Kennedy 2	Liverpool
A. Townsend	Aston Villa
A. Moore	Middlesbrough
N. Quinn	Manchester City

Result 0-2
*Sub: C. Fleming *, L. Daish †*

29th May 1996
v PORTUGAL *Dublin*
S. Given	Blackburn Rovers
C. Fleming	Middlesbrough
T. Phelan	Chelsea
A. Kernaghan +	Manchester City
K. Cunningham	Wimbledon
J. Kenna	Blackburn Rovers
A. Townsend	Aston Villa
A. McLoughlin	Portsmouth
D. Connolly †	Watford
A. Cascarino °	Marseille
G. Farrelly *	Aston Villa

Result 0-1
*Sub: D. Savage *, K. O'Neill †, N. Quinn °, G. Breen +*

26th June 1996
v CROATIA *Dublin*
S. Given	Blackburn Rovers
G. Breen‡	Birmingham City
L. Daish	Coventry City
J. Kenna +	Blackburn Rovers
K. Cunningham°	Wimbledon
A. McLoughlin ^	Portsmouth
M. Kennedy 2	Liverpool
L. O'Brien	Tranmere Rovers
T. Phelan †	Chelsea
N. Quinn	Manchester City
K. O'Neill *	Norwich City

*Result 2-2 K. O'Neill, N. Quinn; Sub: A. Moore *, I. Harte †,*
C. Fleming °, A. Kernaghan +, D. Savage ^, A. Cascarino‡

4th June 1996
v HOLLAND *Rotterdam*
S. Given	Blackburn Rovers
G. Breen	Birmingham City
A. Kernaghan	Manchester City
J. Kenna ^	Blackburn Rovers
I. Harte	Leeds United
L. O'Brien +	Tranmere Rovers
A. McLoughlin	Portsmouth
T. Phelan	Chelsea
A. Moore †	Middlesbrough
D. Connolly °	Watford
A. Cascarino*	Marseille

*Result 1-3 G. Breen; Sub: K. O'Neill *, M. Kennedy 2 †,*
N. Quinn °, K. Cunningham +, C. Fleming ^

9th June 1996
v U.S.A. *Foxboro*
S. Given	Blackburn Rovers
G. Breen	Birmingham City
A. Kernaghan	Manchester City
K. Cunningham	Wimbledon
J. Kenna *	Blackburn Rovers
L. O'Brien +	Tranmere Rovers
G. Farrelly †	Aston Villa
A. McLoughlin	Portsmouth
T. Phelan	Chelsea
N. Quinn °	Manchester City
D. Connolly	Watford

Result 1-2 D. Connolly
*Sub: C. Fleming *, M. Kennedy 2 †, K. O'Neill °, D. Savage +*

12th June 1996
v MEXICO *New Jersey*
P. Bonner	Glasgow Celtic
C. Fleming	Middlesbrough
G. Breen	Birmingham City
L. Daish	Coventry City
I. Harte	Leeds United
M. Kennedy 2 *	Liverpool
D. Savage	Millwall
A. McLoughlin	Portsmouth
A. Moore	Middlesbrough
K. O'Neill	Norwich City
D. Connolly	Watford

Result 2-2 D. Connolly, Davino (og)
*Sub: T. Phelan **

15th June 1996
v BOLIVIA *New Jersey*
S. Given +	Blackburn Rovers
K. Cunningham	Wimbledon
A. Kernaghan *	Manchester City
I. Harte	Leeds United
C. Fleming	Middlesbrough
D. Savage	Millwall
L. O'Brien +	Tranmere Rovers
G. Farrelly °	Aston Villa
T. Phelan	Chelsea
K. O'Neill	Norwich City
A. Moore	Middlesbrough

*Result 3-0 K. O'Neill (2), I. Harte; Sub: G. Breen *,*
A. McLoughlin †, M. Kennedy 2 °, P. Bonner +

SOCCER BOOK PUBLISHING LTD.
72 ST. PETER'S AVENUE
CLEETHORPES
N.E. LINCOLNSHIRE
DN35 8HU
Phone (01472) 696226
FAX (01472) 698546

BACK NUMBERS

We still have the undermentioned publications available post free at the reduced prices shown. There are very few remaining copies of some of these titles so, please, order any that you require without delay to avoid disappointment.

Year	TITLE	Price	Qty	Order Value
1990	The Supporters' Guide to Football League Clubs 1991	£2.95		
1991	The Supporters' Guide to Football League Clubs 1992	£3.99		
1992	The Supporters' Guide to Football League Clubs 1993	£3.99		
1992	The Supporters' Guide to Scottish Football 1993	£2.99		
1993	The Supporters' Guide to Premier & Football League Clubs 1994	£3.99		
1993	The Supporters' Guide to Scottish Football 1994	£3.99		
1993	The Supporters' Guide to Welsh Football 1994	£3.99		
1994	The Supporters' Guide to Premier & Football League Clubs 1995	£3.99		
1994	The Supporters' Guide to Scottish Football 1995	£3.99		
1994	The Supporters' Guide to Non-League Football 1995	£3.99		
1994	The Supporters' Guide to Welsh Football 1995	£3.99		
1995	The Supporters' Guide to Premier & Football League Clubs 1996	£3.99		
1995	The Supporters' Guide to Scottish Football 1996	£3.99		
1995	The Supporters' Guide to Non-League Football 1996	£3.99		
1995	The Supporters' Guide to Welsh Football 1996	£3.99		
1995	The Supporters' Guide to Football Programmes 1996	£3.99		

THE 25 YEAR RECORD SERIES

Top quality 25 season histories with line-ups, results, scorers, attendances and season-by-season write-ups.

Titles currently available...

Chelsea F.C. .... Seasons 1971-72 to 1995-
Middlesbrough F.C. .... Seasons 1971-72 to 1995-
Preston North End F.C. .... Seasons 1971-72 to 1995-
Southampton F.C. .... Seasons 1971-72 to 1995-
Sunderland F.C. .... Seasons 1971-72 to 1995-

Aston Villa F.C. .... Seasons 1970-71 to 1994-
Celtic F.C. .... Seasons 1970-71 to 1994-
Derby County F.C. .... Seasons 1970-71 to 1994-
Everton F.C. .... Seasons 1970-71 to 1994-
Leeds United F.C. .... Seasons 1970-71 to 1994-
Liverpool F.C. .... Seasons 1970-71 to 1994-
Manchester United F.C. .... Seasons 1970-71 to 1994-
Newcastle United F.C. .... Seasons 1970-71 to 1994-
Nottingham Forest F.C. .... Seasons 1970-71 to 1994-
Rangers F.C. .... Seasons 1970-71 to 1994-

Also available (no write-ups):
Burnley F.C. .... Seasons 1969-70 to 1993-

All titles are softback and priced £4.99

Available post free from:

Soccer Book Publishing Ltd. (Dept. SBP)
72 St. Peter's Avenue
Cleethorpes
N.E. Lincolnshire
DN35 8HU

Tel. (01472) 601893
Fax (01472) 698546